Dietrich
Bonhoeffer

MODERN SPIRITUAL MASTERS
Robert Ellsberg, Series Editor

This series introduces the writing and vision of some of the great spiritual masters of the twentieth century. Along with selections from their writings, each volume includes a comprehensive introduction, presenting the author's life and writings in context, and drawing attention to points of special relevance to contemporary spirituality.

Some of these authors found a wide audience in their lifetimes. In other cases recognition has come long after their deaths. Some are rooted in long-established traditions of spirituality. Others charted new, untested paths. In each case, however, the authors in this series have engaged in a spiritual journey shaped by the influences and concerns of our age. Such concerns include the challenges of modern science, religious pluralism, secularism, and the quest for social justice.

At the dawn of a new millennium this series commends these modern spiritual masters, along with the saints and witnesses of previous centuries, as guides and companions to a new generation of seekers.

Already published:
Simone Weil (edited by Eric O. Springsted)
Henri Nouwen (edited by Robert A. Jonas)

Forthcoming volumes include:
Pierre Teilhard de Chardin
Karl Rahner
Oscar Romero
John Main
Flannery O'Connor
Brother Roger of Taizé

DIETRICH BONHOEFFER

Writings Selected
with an Introduction by
ROBERT COLES

ORBIS BOOKS
Maryknoll, New York 10545

The Catholic Foreign Mission Society of America (Maryknoll) recruits and trains people for overseas missionary service. Through Orbis Books, Maryknoll aims to foster the international dialogue that is essential to mission. The books published, however, reflect the opinions of their authors and are not meant to represent the official position of the society.

Manufactured in the United States of America

Library of Congress Cataloging-in-Publication Data
Bonhoeffer, Dietrich, 1906–1945.
    [Selections. English. 1998]
    Dietrich Bonhoeffer / writings selected with an introduction by Robert Coles.
    p.   cm. – (Modern spiritual masters series)
    Includes bibliographical references.
    ISBN 1-57075-194-3 (pbk.)
    1. Theology. I. Coles, Robert. II. Title. III. Series.
BX4827.B57A25 1998
230′044 – dc21
                                             98-26303

Contents

Preface

These writings are meant to convey a sense of a mid-twentieth-century Christian pilgrim's journey — from brilliant, scholarly essays to a martyr's last thoughts, prophecies, speculations. As with any of us, there were several Bonhoeffers, and his life's work can therefore be regarded in different ways by various readers. The point of this selection is to indicate a certain spiritual theme or direction that (with heightening realization as he grew older) informs all his books, correspondence, and lectures, an aspect of his being that, in retrospect, we know to have been utterly crucial for him — and revelatory for the rest of us.

Even in his early years as a religious philosopher, a young, aspiring theologian, Dietrich Bonhoeffer dared to struggle in the boldest way with matters of spirituality, of faith. In 1930, at twenty-four, he was looking to the future — but not that of worldly success. The "future" he contemplates in *Act and Being* is one of Christ's embrace — an anticipation that for him is not to be equated with the contemplation or reflection he had learned to do so well as a scholar. Already, long before he would take on the "principalities and powers" of his fearfully fallen nation, he was ready to take on an especially seductive form of egoism: the knowing self thoroughly intent on analyzing what has happened, what is happening. Alternately, he urges on all of us a leap into Christ's arms, as if He were a parent, and we His once errant but now hopeful and trusting children. This emphasis on the future and its possible promise is, of course, so achingly ironic, given what awaited the author of *Act and Being* only a few years down the line.

In 1933, such a fateful year for Germany, for the whole world, even as Hitler was consolidating his hold as Germany's chancellor, Bonhoeffer the teacher was giving lectures at the University of Berlin (from May to July), published as *Christ the Center.* In those lectures he called upon Jesus in a most personal and searching way, as if, already, he knew what was about to happen: a nation's institutionalized religion (the Lutheran Church) become the property of a bunch of killers. Bonhoeffer's broad humanism, his ease with literature, his willingness to connect faith with the lived life, and his insistence that the spiritual is not to be confused with the intellectual (or the material or the conventional, the popular, the socially acceptable) is again, ironic, in view of what would soon enough come around the corner of his young life: secular power claiming unlimited sanction (and getting it from pastors and priests galore).

By 1937, when Bonhoeffer wrote *The Cost of Discipleship,* Germany had been duped, tricked, seduced, and seized by the Devil. Nazi rule was beyond effective challenge, and humiliation was everywhere: the humiliation of the Jews, the humiliation of those still loyal to democratic values, and, yes, the humiliation of the professors and doctors and lawyers and churchmen (so-called Christians) who had flocked to the swastika, wore it boldly, asserted its proclamations and purposes. Under such circumstances, worthy of comparison to the darkest hours in the life of Jesus, a new Dietrich Bonhoeffer was born. Now, the theologian (who had prophetically, if intellectually, written of the "future" of "act," of "being," of Christ's lived example as the heart of things, as, finally, the *all* for any of us who claims allegiance to Christianity) would become Kierkegaard's "Knight of Faith," tested not by his performances in academic conferences, not by the response of critics of his articles and books, not by the judgment of his theological colleagues, but by his willingness to refuse the blandishments of Nazi rule; to stand up to unparalleled power; to stand for Him of the Galilean sayings when others flocked to shout "Heil" at Nuremberg; to stand alone, in prison, and finally, to stand before the guns of the murderous deputies of a latter-day Roman empire exerting one of its last vengeful acts.

Bonhoeffer the devout, erudite Lutheran was on his way to becoming something else than a church-going scholar and writer and university lecturer. Bonhoeffer sought Christ's companionship, a "discipleship" that does, indeed, come at a high "cost." Now the "life together" that Bonhoeffer so earnestly tried to find was one in a "community" headed by Jesus rather than this or that secular authority. Now, the "ethics" of which he wrote became a direct challenge to everything espoused by his country's leaders and their all too evidently compliant followers, who by the tens of millions were streaming (while ranting) toward a collective moral suicide. Now, in prison, a man condemned, he would find his "future" all right, would find a "christology" of the suffering flesh, would learn the steep personal "cost" of a Christian allegiance practiced daily, would find a "life together" with his Lord in a prison cell's solitariness, would grope amid terrible darkness for an ethics of "love," of "success" that faced down unstintingly, unreservedly the officialdom of a devilish regime.

In prison, Bonhoeffer wrote poetry; in prison he sang of a Christianity liberated from the military boot of a contemporary anti-Christ, and of a spirituality sprung from ponderous theology and prideful ecclesiastical dogma. In prison he addressed his beloved Savior through an "act" (resistance to Nazi might) become a steadfast believer's "being," through a constantly embraced Christ as the "center" of his life, through a lived and ever so costly "discipleship," through a "life together" with Him, through an "ethics" of love and success utterly topsy-turvy in nature when compared to what prevailed around him, and finally, through letters and diaries that tell of a humbled pilgrim's most exemplary and passionate and worthy ascent toward God — walked in a cell, on the grounds of jail or one concentration camp after another: amid hell the sight of heaven, of Jesus the chosen comrade, the beckoning companion.

Acknowledgments

1. "Jesus Christ and the Essence of Christianity": Address delivered in Barcelona on December 11, 1928. Translation reprinted from Geffrey B. Kelly and F. Burton Nelson, eds., *A Testament to Freedom: The Essential Writings of Dietrich Bonhoeffer* (New York: HarperCollins, 1990). Copyright © 1991 by Geffrey B. Kelly and F. Burton Nelson. Reprinted by permission of HarperCollins Publishers, Inc.

2. From the introduction to *Christ the Center,* rev. trans. Edwin H. Robertson (New York: Harper & Row, 1978). English translation copyright © 1966 by William Collins, Sons & Co., Ltd. and Harper & Row Publishers, Inc. Reprinted by permission of HarperCollins Publishers, Inc.

3. Selections from *The Cost of Discipleship* by Dietrich Bonhoeffer, trans. R. H. Fuller with some revision by Irmgard Booth (New York: Macmillan, 1963). Reprinted with the permission of Simon & Schuster. Copyright © 1959 by SCM Press, Ltd.

4. Selections from *Life Together,* trans. John Doberstein (New York: Harper & Row, 1954). English translation copyright © 1954 by Harper & Brothers, copyright renewed 1982 by Helen S. Doberstein. Reprinted by permission of HarperCollins Publishers, Inc.

5. "Pastor of the Confessing Church": Selections reprinted from Geffrey B. Kelly and F. Burton Nelson, eds., *A Testament to Freedom: The Essential Writings of Dietrich Bonhoeffer* (New York: HarperCollins, 1990). Copyright © 1991 by Geffrey B. Kelly and F. Burton Nelson. Reprinted by permission of HarperCollins Publishers, Inc.

6. Selections from *Ethics,* ed. Eberhard Bethge, trans. Neville Horton Smith (New York: Macmillan, 1955). Reprinted with the permission of Simon & Schuster. Copyright © 1955 by Mac-

11

Moments in Dietrich Bonhoeffer's Life

1906   Born in Breslau, Germany, on February 4, the son of Karl Bonhoeffer, a distinguished neuropsychiatrist, and Paula (Von Hase) Bonhoeffer, of a prominent family.

1912   Bonhoeffer family takes up residence in Berlin.

1923   Begins religious and theological studies at Tübingen University.

1924   Begins further theological studies at Berlin University.

1927   Completes work for doctoral degree. Thesis is titled "The Communion of Saints."

1928   Goes to Barcelona, Spain, as a curate in a Lutheran church.

1930   Finishes *Act and Being*. In September goes to Union Theological Seminary in New York City as a Sloan Fellow.

1931   Becomes lecturer in theology at Berlin University. Ordained a minister in the Lutheran Church.

1933   On February 1, two days after Hitler was made chancellor, broadcasts on the radio a warning about totalitarianism and is cut off the air as he speaks. In September joins with Pastor Martin Niemöller in addressing Germany's ministers with respect to the moral dangers of Nazi rule.

1934   Helps organize the Confessing Church, a critical response to Hitler and also to the Lutheran Church, which, by and large, had quickly deferred to, then embraced the Nazis.

13

1935   Teaches at Seminary for the Confessing Church at Finkenwalde (near Stettin). In December the Nazis begin to curb activities at the seminary.

1936   Bonhoeffer no longer permitted to teach at Berlin University.

1937   Seminary at Finkenwalde closed by the Gestapo. *The Cost of Discipleship* published.

1938   Establishes contact with political opponents of Hitler. Now forbidden to do pastoral work or teach in Berlin. Works on *Life Together*.

1939   Goes to England. Shares his anxieties about and for his native land with ministers and theologians in London. Visits the United States again, but within weeks returns to Germany, much to the worried dismay of his American friends.

1940   Prohibited from making public speeches, watched closely by the police. Writes part of *Ethics*. Visits Benedictine monastery near Munich.

1941   Visits Switzerland, but returns to Germany, where he is under heavy suspicion by Nazi authorities.

1942   Travels abroad again, to Norway, Sweden, and Switzerland. Meets with friends from England and elsewhere.

1943   Becomes engaged to Maria von Wedemeyer; three months later he is arrested and put in Berlin's Tegel Prison.

1944   Moved from Tegel Prison to Gestapo prison in Berlin. His brother Klaus and brother-in-law Rüdiger Schleicher are arrested. (They are killed in 1945.)

1945   Moved to Buchenwald concentration camp, then to Regensburg camp, then to Schönberg, and finally Flossenbürg, where he is court-martialed and, on April 9, executed.

Introduction

The Making of a Disciple

The heart of Christianity, obviously, is God's willingness to become a man, to live in a particular place and time, to enter history, experience its possibilities and constraints, test their limits: Jesus the Jewish child born in Bethlehem, a town that belonged to the Roman empire, and later Jesus the carpenter, then the teacher and healer and itinerant preacher, and ultimately, the insistent reformer distrusted by religious and political officialdom to the point that he is seized, condemned, and killed. Jesus lived only thirty-three years; his closest friends were humble folk, fishermen and peasants, even men and women who had known pain, had transgressed laws, had lived vulnerable, improvident, or unchaste lives. Nor was he immediately, upon his agonizing, humiliating death, recognized by the multitude as the long awaited messiah of Jewish yearning. Even as his closest comrades had all abandoned him in life, only a handful were ready to rally around him, initially, in death. Here, again, he had to come to terms with history. His ideas and pronouncements, the memory of him in others, became in their sum an aspect of a political moment, a religious and social and cultural one: an era's evolving struggles with respect to what is believed by whom, and with which consequences. The story of the eventual triumph of Christianity within the confines of Roman power, and then beyond it, is also the story of many martyrs who were not reluctant to undergo persecution, to be tortured and killed, all in the name of a professed faith. Moreover, the above drama of God as historical protagonist (of Christ become someone followed or opposed, embraced at whatever cost in what He urged, or merely acknowledged with lip service, or refuted and ridiculed) is still enacted. The Jesus of the first century has become the Christ who has figured in all the centuries thereafter, certainly including this one of ours, now coming to a close: two millennia of believers and skeptics and martyrs — all of them, in different ways, shaped by the historical circumstances that informed their lives.

Christianity is also a religion of surprises — its entrance into history the biggest, but there have been many others along the way. Jesus as a boy surprised his elders in the Temple by his precocity, and when he was a young carpenter his wisdom startled, dazzled others, some of them big-shots, others ordinary folk who have always had very good reason to distrust those who have come with promise. Imperial Rome may have had its discontents, but surely the spread of Christianity through its various precincts was a most unexpected outcome, a stunning instance of an obscure band of lowly people who lived in a remote part of a mighty realm generating a faith that in a few generations became an institutional presence of enormous authority and power. Nor have those surprises failed to arrive at Christianity's door ever since — from the failed papacy of Celestine V, the Benedictine monk who as an old man was brought to the church's throne, only to stumble badly, his virtues and exemplary piety no help at all in dealing with the demands of institutional politics, to the papacy of John XXIII in our time; and from the emergence of John Calvin, of Martin Luther in Europe, to the founding and growth of America, in no small measure a consequence of Christian passions finding their expression and resolution in trans-Atlantic travel, in the exploration and the settlement in a new continent.

So, too, with the life of Dietrich Bonhoeffer: who, knowing him as a child, a young man, even a young Lutheran pastor and theologian, would have predicted the course of his life, its terrible foreshortening? He died (on April 9, 1945) in a German prison, killed as a convicted traitor to his country. He was only thirty-nine. And surely upon his birth (on February 4, 1906) or during his childhood and youth, such an outcome was beyond anyone's wildest imagining. Some men and women show early signs of talent and, too, of interests and qualities of temperament that, in retrospect, have all signaled the direction, if not denouncement, of their lives — especially if one looks at their family background as well. But Bonhoeffer, like so many others, came to be the person we now know and admire only in response to history's hard-to-predict unfolding. In a sense, after all, his moral testing, his spiritual fate, which so distinguished him from so many others, including thousands of Germany's Christian ministers, had everything to do with the triumph of Adolf Hitler and his Nazi thugs. And as the Yale historian Henry Ashby Turner, Jr., has recently shown us, their political victory, in late January of 1933, was far from inevitable; it was, rather, a tragic result of betrayals, lies, deceptions, and deals that bewildered and staggered most of Germany's voters (a majority of whom had rejected the shrill, Austrian-born hate-monger).

How then do we understand the life of Dietrich Bonhoeffer, and especially the way in which it came to an end? Even as Hitler's rise to power was not inevitable, Bonhoeffer's arrest, imprisonment, and death were not the unavoidable conclusion to a religious (or ideological or psychological or social and cultural) drama. They could not have been foreseen by, say, 1933, with Hitler's ascent to power, or even in 1940, with his military victories evident and his authority at home a living nightmare for many — who, still, found ways of staying clear of the Gestapo, surviving the war, speaking with dignity and credibility to their fellow Germans, as Konrad Adenauer did. Indeed, in certain respects Bonhoeffer was an unlikely candidate for the role he eventually assumed, that of a principled fighter unto death against the German state. He was, after all, a Lutheran, for whom a nation's government deserves enormous respect, a matter of doctrine. Luther's emergence, ironically, had everything to do with just that matter; what he preached in that regard served the interests of rising secular leaders, anxious to be free of Rome's claimed rights over them. Nor had Bonhoeffer grown up in a politically radical or culturally cosmopolitan home. His mother was from a renowned, accomplished family, whose members included a minister who belonged to the kaiser's court and a high military official, as well as lawyers and businessmen, titled members of the nobility. And similarly, his father was one of Germany's leading neuropsychiatrists, even as his relatives included jurists and individuals of the *haute bourgeoisie*. Dietrich was born in Breslau, but when he was six his father assumed an important position in Berlin, though, again, for all the intellectual ferment in the capital city, especially during the years of the Weimar Republic, the Bonhoeffers stood apart: a solid, stable, well-to-do family protected by its own largely secular values as well as its Lutheran loyalties from the moral and political skepticism that flourished in various Berlin circles and salons.

Dietrich Bonhoeffer was one of eight children. His oldest brother, Karl-Friedrich, would become a physicist. His older brother Walter was killed in the German army during the First World War. His brother Klaus, three years older, would become a lawyer — and would stand up to the Nazis, and be jailed and killed by them. His older sisters, Ursula and Christine, both married lawyers (Rüdiger Schleicher and Hans von Dohnanyi) who also passionately resisted Hitler's henchmen, and they too were arrested and killed just before the war ended. Bonhoeffer's twin sister, Sabine, married a lawyer and political scientist, Gerhard Leibholz, who was of Jewish ancestry, although a baptized Christian, and his youngest sister, Susanne, married Walter Press, a theologian. This was a family that lost four members to the Nazis, a moral resistance of a high order. The family also "lost" a daughter and son-in-law to exile in 1935, as the Nazis bore down relentlessly and viciously on anyone of Jewish background. Yet it was not a family whose interests and convictions, before the rise of Hitler, would seem to make it an all-out antagonist of his, ready to fight him (as the saying goes, and as it would happen) "unto death."

Hitler, actually, did not lack opponents who were of upper-class background, conservative in many respects, nationalistic, even (alas) anti-Semitic in their own quieter, more genteel fashion. The Nazis were by and large riff-raff; and initially their appeal was to people who, despite their social and economic vulnerability, disdained and feared the left — the Weimar Republic's substantial socialist and communist presence. Hitler proclaimed *national* "socialism," a demagogic "populism" that offered the old consolations and satisfactions of hate: the Jew as the explanatory scapegoat. For certain upper-class Germans, connected to law and business and the military, Hitler's coarseness (and the crudities of his Nazi gauleiters) was obviously distasteful. A loose American analogy would be the contempt certain well-off, well-educated American Southerners had for the Klan, even as those same individuals had no interest at all in seeing blacks obtain even political (never mind social or economic) equality.

With Hitler's rise, needless to say, not only the Jews had to come to terms with what he stood for and, step by step, what he aimed to do and, very energetically, insisted on doing. Even many Jews thought power would tame Hitler, subdue his hysterical ranting, and curb the activity of his violence-prone followers. As for Germany's "Aryan" population, including its avowedly Christian members, Catholic and Protestant alike, it was soon enough effectively subdued by a totalitarian regime which brooked no opposition and got its way as it confronted anyone's doubts or misgivings with the full thrust of political power and with all that such control can do to exert its will. In fact, the quick accommodation of Germany's Protestant churches to Hitler tells volumes about the role of religion in the secular life of a twentieth-century industrial nation. Just as important was the role of the universities, for they too quickly made an amicable settlement with Hitler. In no time faculties were purged, books condemned and burned, and a host of leading intellectuals and their followers became public accomplices to or apologists for Nazi ideology. Or, more quietly, they fell in line with no inclination to express disagreement or qualms. Lawyers, journalists, physicians, teachers, ministers in droves became willing instruments of Hitler's various functionaries. Hundreds of ministers, on occasion, wore the Nazi brown shirt, embracing the Führer's leadership. In contrast, within days of Hitler's ascension as chancellor, Bonhoeffer spoke up, took on Nazism as idolatrous, spoke in defense of the Jews, and warned strenuously against the direction his nation was going — and in so doing, was cut off, actually, in the midst of a radio address.

How to account for such an early resistance, publicly expressed? In 1933 Dietrich Bonhoeffer was a twenty-seven-year-old pastor and theologian residing in Berlin and connected to university life as a teacher and a minister. He had become, already, a promising theologian: he had gone to Spain to minister to a German-speaking population in Barcelona, and he had spent a year at New York City's Union Theological Seminary. No question, he had already shown substantial evidence of a compassionate nature. In Barcelona, his heart went out to the working people, the unemployed in a nation even then contending with the conflicts that would bring to the fore Francisco Franco, one of Hitler's major allies. In America, Bonhoeffer would right away take note of *our* institutional racism (in 1930, before Hitler had come to power). He worried long and hard about a nation that segregated millions of its citizens, keeping them both apart and below: an affront, he saw clearly, to the readily espoused Christianity of those who, nevertheless, had no apparent trouble with such a racial situation.

Yet, in other respects, he was obviously (at Union Theological Seminary, certainly) an almost quaintly conservative young visitor from abroad. Whereas the social gospel dominated the discourse at the seminary — the Great Depression was in full sway then — this young Lutheran of obviously genteel background was (at least intellectually) more interested in God than in man. Like Karl Barth, whom he admired, Bonhoeffer tried to comprehend what he acknowledged to be, finally, incomprehensible: God's reasons and ways. It is in our nature to do just that, to try to ascertain whatever we can of the Divine — and maybe all we can do is describe our yearning to do so, the futility of our search, and, perhaps, speculate on His will and even on His interests or wishes. The austerity (if not fancy) of such a posture must surely have struck some at Union Seminary (well into the twentieth century, after Darwin and Marx and Freud and Einstein, no less, not to mention the seeming worldwide collapse of capitalism) as remarkable, and not without social, cultural, and psychological implications: a flight to the unfathomable God of John Calvin as an alternative to an embrace of God's creatures, here at hand, in their all too obvious and profound suffering.

Not that Bonhoeffer himself was indifferent to the world of the here and now. He was an immensely likable, earnest man whose moral energy and evidently compassionate nature enabled him to get on well, indeed, with his American hosts. A devout Lutheran, he bowed to God's distant, unshakable power; a decent, approachable human being of good instincts and fine sensibility, he worried about his neighbors, of whatever kind, creed, or color. At Union, Bonhoeffer became especially close to Paul Lehmann, but to others as well; he carried them in his mind and soul. He corresponded with them throughout the dark days ahead, in the 1930s, and saw them all too briefly, at the end of that decade, just before the Second World War began.

Back in Germany Bonhoeffer would soon enough say goodbye to the life of the young, promising theologian, the university-connected pastor and teacher and scholar, the Berliner of impeccable social background who played the piano brilliantly and who had also learned to play a very good game of tennis, whose family, amid the economic chaos of the 1920s, had never known the jeopardy, the doubts and anxieties, that descended on middle-class people, never mind the poor. Such people by the millions had turned to the communists or the Nazis, who were not only electoral opponents, but engaged in a fierce, unremitting battle for the streets of a proud, highly educated, industrial (and industrious) nation on the verge of political as well as economic collapse. On January 30, 1933, as a consequence of endless bargaining and manipulations behind closed doors, the very worst, the unthinkable happened. Hitler, on that day, became Germany's chancellor, and the fate of millions and millions of people the world over became sealed: for one reason or another they would be killed in the next twelve years, among them the then twenty-seven-year-old Bonhoeffer, who immediately made public his opposition to the Nazis.

Not that Bonhoeffer (or anyone else) knew how far in the direction of absolute evil the Nazis would take Germany and all of

Europe. But he took a more accurate measure of those murderous thugs than others, and began to do so right away. He was, as mentioned, cut off speaking on the radio days after Hitler took office as he warned of the idolatry that would accompany the constant din of "Führer." Day by day, month by month, the Nazis engineered their totalitarian hold on the nation, and with it the flagrant racialism of anti-Semitism — a terrible echo, alas, that hearkened back over the centuries to, among others, Luther himself. But now those distant denunciations and, more recently, the Wagnerian descents into a self-importance that was purchased at the expense of others became something quite else: a state-sponsored hate with a killing aim. While his fellow ministers flocked to the Führer, Bonhoeffer and a relative handful of others became part of the "Confessing Church": on their knees they begged God's forgiveness for what was being said and done in their native land, even as they knew they themselves were risking their own situations, if not lives, by so doing. It was a time of great testing, a time when some fled, others submitted, still others began what would be the march of many millions to the concentration camps, the factories of murder that only an "advanced" technology in a nation such as Germany could enable and sustain.

Late in 1933 Bonhoeffer left Germany again, now for England. His opposition to the Nazis was clear and publicly known, but perhaps he needed time to figure out how he would enact it. Meanwhile, the Nazis accelerated their cultural (never mind political) control over Germany, so that when Bonhoeffer returned in 1935, the kind of work he did — the training of ministers in a tradition of prayerful opposition to the values being daily propounded by the Nazis and pounded into the minds of the German people under the adroit guidance of Joseph Goebbels — had become exceedingly dangerous. Nevertheless, in 1935, a Preachers' Seminary had opened, located first at Zingshof, on the Baltic Sea, and then at Finkenwalde, near Stettin. There, during the last years of Auden's "low, dishonest decade," wherein hell itself began summoning the German people, Bonhoeffer and a few others gathered, prayed, studied, and prepared themselves for what they must have surely sensed to be around the corner in their lives. Whereas the great majority of Lutheran pastors consented to Hitler's rule, even welcomed it and wore the swastika on occasion, Bonhoeffer and his associates said no to such an accommodation, if not an embrace. Instead they initiated a "Confessing Church," one at odds with established Christian officialdom. It was during these few years that Bonhoeffer wrote *The Cost of Discipleship* (1937) and *Life Together* (1939). In a way, he was divesting himself of the Lutheran legacy of a state-connected church and radically attaching himself to Jesus, who for him was now very much a living, constant ethical and spiritual guide. Even as Germany's clergy had become the Führer's self-abased "disciples," Bonhoeffer was exhorting his friends, his moral companions at Finkenwalde, to stand fast with Jesus Christ, with all He upheld and passed on to others, His disciples. The "cost" would be a fearful isolation, a growing ostracism. But all in that community, all sharing that "life together," had already realized not only the intent of the Nazis, but their absolute determination to fulfill their own expectations at all costs. Hence the "cost" Bonhoeffer had in mind for himself and others like him: death if necessary, in pursuit of a committed Christian life.

By 1939 it had become clear that there was no stopping Hitler at home or, indeed, abroad, short of another world war. England and France had seen their desperate sell-out of Czechoslovakia at Munich come to naught. Now the Nazi beast was growling ferociously at Poland, and those two countries were feverishly preparing for the inevitable confrontation. At this point Bonhoeffer made his second visit to the United States. At Union Seminary he was a changed person: he had already been tested morally and personally the way few at that seminary, or any of us, get to be. He hadn't resisted Hitler in articles and signed petitions written in distant lands, in sermons delivered way out of the reach of the (even then) notorious Gestapo; rather, he had made crystal clear his principles within visiting distance of the Gestapo. Moreover, no sooner was he safely in America in June of 1939 than he was determined to return; he did so in July. Weeks later World War II would start, and his American friends would worry and wonder: why that hasty return, given the resistance he would offer and the consequent retaliatory response?

In this regard I remember well a conversation with Reinhold and Ursula Niebuhr in the summer of 1963 and their polite but candid wish to convey not only the concern so many at Union Seminary felt for Bonhoeffer, but an interesting and all too instructive variant of that concern. Why did he want so badly to go back to Germany? What did the "homesickness" of which he frequently spoke "really" mean? Was he not, perhaps, "depressed"? Might not he have been helped by some "conversations" with a "professional" person? Wouldn't it have been "wiser" for him to stay in America and help rouse a significantly isolationist nation to an awareness of what was at stake in Europe? By then Paul Tillich and Karl Barth had gone into exile; hadn't Bonhoeffer already struggled harder against the Nazis than just about anyone throughout the German universities, throughout Christendom? To their arbitrary, overwhelming, unscrupulous state power he had dared (by not so subtle or indirect gestures) to say a resounding no. Before his second visit to America his friends abroad already saw jail coming for him, if not worse, and they were pleased when, at last, he had crossed the Atlantic on a visit they hoped would necessarily become an extended stay. He would never give an explicit account of his reasons for a return in the summer of 1939. He cited "homesickness," but more to the point he let Reinhold Niebuhr know that if he were to have any future credibility and moral worth to his countrymen after Hitler's defeat, he would need to have been part of the struggle that earned that defeat: "I must live through this difficult period of our national history with the Christian people of Germany. I will have no right to participate in the reconstruction of Christian life in Germany after the war if I do not share the trials of this time with my people." A sentiment of someone looking to the future with hope; a sentiment of someone who surely wanted to live, to pay freely and fully "the cost of discipleship," but also to have a chance to share in a coming redemptive moment.

Once back in Germany he could not help seeing an implied meaning of the "homesickness" he suffered in New York City:

his "home" was fatally "sick." With Germany at war all hin-
drances to Nazi bestiality were lifted. The Nazi juggernaut across
one national border after another was accompanied by a determination to pursue the wholesale murder of the Jews and of
all others deemed "inferior" or "enemies" by a regime that was
revealing itself, steadily, to be so monstrously evil as to have
no parallel in all history. Bonhoeffer the resistor now plunged
onward, the anti-Christ all around him. Through family connections he joined the Abwehr, the Military Intelligence, which for a
while was secure from Gestapo surveillance. Thereby he did not
have to fight in Hitler's legions, and thereby he in fact became a
double agent, ostensibly working for Germany while he was plot-
ting as best he could the defeat of Hitler. We are here in several
senses on territory best described by Graham Greene or perhaps
Joseph Conrad — the singular moral passion of someone who
challenged conventional morality in its established political expression. Bonhoeffer's fellow subversives were his brother Klaus,
his two brothers-in-law, and an assortment of military officials,
diplomats, and aristocrats — each with a particular lifetime's reasons to take such a radical and extremely dangerous step. To
be sure, some were not without blemishes — old-school Junkers,
army and navy men who wanted a powerful Germany but not
one run by a raving hater who was threatening to bring down
anyone and everyone who disagreed with his views and those of
his low-life associates: a great nation become a gangster nation.

For Bonhoeffer, there was this huge religious irony: a Lutheran, he was now no longer in nominal opposition to the state;
he was trying with all his might to lay it low — and in time,
he would be arrested, imprisoned, and killed just days before
Hitler's suicide. Even as Allied artillery and airplanes caused the
ground where his prison stood to shake, he prayed, ministered
unto others, and went to his death with a stoicism unforgettable
to those who witnessed it. For him, surely, this was a "cost of
discipleship" not discussed in writing, analyzed in arguments,
worked into a polemical position, but assumed in the course of
an intensely spiritual life. He was nearing his fortieth birthday
and engaged to be married. The Nazis murdered him and others

as a last gasp; within a month Germany (such as it then was) surrendered unconditionally to the Allied forces. One can only imagine what it was like, amid the ruins of Berlin, for Dr. and Mrs. Bonhoeffer and for Maria von Wedemeyer, their son Dietrich's fiancée (who had lost her father and two brothers to the war), to learn that he and his brother and his two brothers-in-law had been put to death during the last moments of the war.

The Devil came to Germany (through a devilish politics) in 1933, and this was not a Devil who came in slippery shoes, as the saying goes. Rather, this was a full-fledged, undisguised, head-on, modern, secular, statist version: mass murder become routine across the most "civilized" continent, in the cradle of historical Christianity — "the Rome-Berlin axis," as it was then known. Bonhoeffer's distinctive spirituality, that of a daily enactment of the moral truths spoken by Jesus and worked into His life, is our legacy (the terrible irony!) courtesy of that utterly devastating horror. Adolf Hitler gave us the Dietrich Bonhoeffer we admire and venerate today, a half century and more after his death at the hands of a Nazi executioner. "Prisoner Bonhoeffer, get ready and come with us," he was told by those who would soon thereafter kill him. And with that deed he "came" to all of "us." A long witness, a chosen ordeal at last ended — only to have a new existence, not only the heavenly one for which he aspired when he spoke the last words known to us ("This is the end — for me the beginning of life"), but the earthly one in which generations after him have shared. He was a man of faith now celebrated, his moral will such that it defied the dozens of evasions and rationalizations and self-justifications to which the rest of us are only too obviously and frequently heir. No question, to repeat, this man whose memory we continue to honor could have had it otherwise. He might still be with us, a revered and wise theologian and teacher, a one-time anti-Nazi activist, now in his early nineties, a person of intellectual achievement and moral stature.

George Eliot said farewell, unforgettably, at the end of *Middlemarch* (to the individuals whose complexity of mind and heart she had so subtly rendered) with these words: "Who can quit young lives after being long in company with them, and not desire to know what befell them in their after-years? For the fragment of a life, however typical, is not the sample of an even web: promises may not be kept, and an ardent onset may be followed by declension; latent powers may find their long-waited opportunity; a past error may urge a grand retrieval." Here is a shrewdly capacious psychology accounting for a secular dialectic in all its possibilities. Yet in Bonhoeffer we see little of the zig and zag so aptly evoked by a masterful observer of human psychology. In Bonhoeffer's life the march of his feet, step upon step, is directed, relentless, all too foretellable, an insistent and persistent and resounding antiphon of dissent to the legions of hate that paraded across Germany, then other countries: murder in constant motion (the whole world watching) inflicted by the militarily empowered dregs of our species. To such a fearsome anti-Christ, a would-be "disciple" of Jesus proved himself just that — and so, once more, the crucifixion story. By then Hitler was already in his bunker, on his way, one can only hope, to a future that even the greatest surveyor of our past and future, Dante, could never have imagined.

In his early twenties Bonhoeffer seemed headed for a distinguished career as a Lutheran pastor and teacher who also was called to ponder and write theology. He was eminently loyal to the notion of authority and hierarchy, of faith as something handed down in great mystery from above (rather than found and explored within oneself). For Lutherans the state is, really, an aspect of God's divinity granted us from on high; Christianity is a body of beliefs and convictions that is integrated into one's daily life as a burgher, a citizen, a member of an established community. The courthouse is not a church, but they share space in a town's center, and they are meant to inform each other's everyday life. Christ's declaration with respect to Caesar and God is regarded as a dual or joint mandate rather than an admonishing rebuke of an intrusive civil authority — a plea to believers that they keep a safe distance between their political responsibilities and their practiced religious life.

Not that Lutherans are completely bound to institutional compliance. Theirs is, needless to say, a Protestant faith. Their

founder took on Roman Catholicism, insisting on his right
and, by implication, anyone's right to seek God in the private
ways of prayer, but also in reflection, discussion, and argument.
Lutheranism posits civil commitment as an expression of the
religious life, but it frees the individual worshiper from the in-
tercessory role of popes and cardinals. And so each of us has a
private leeway with respect to our faith, though we also belong
to a family, a neighborhood, and a nation. If Luther transferred
some papal power to the pastors and some to the "principalities" to which those pastors belonged, he left the individual
parishioner a certain private territory wherein God is encountered (imagined, considered, beseeched) with no one necessarily
looking over one's shoulder. Hence the orthodoxy, as it were, of
Bonhoeffer's notion of a God far more private and inscrutable
than many Christians, of whatever denomination, would have
Him be.

While the young Bonhoeffer of the 1920s was reminding
himself and his readers that faith requires submission to the significantly unknowable, even the unapproachable, he was also
simply taking for granted the political system that then prevailed
in his native land — a conventional Lutheran state of mind (or
soul). That is to say, he was not caught up in the considerable
tensions of Weimar Germany. He lived a sheltered, scholarly life
and broke with it not at home, but abroad, in Spain. Thereafter
he journeyed to America, where (again) the churches were much
involved in the social and economic struggles of a faltering capitalism. To be sure, from the distance of those two journeys he
would become aware of new pastoral possibilities — the minister
as a political or social critic and, if necessary, activist. But until
Paul Hindenberg gave Hitler the office he'd been seeking for a
decade, Bonhoeffer had shown no signs of any great interest in
his exceedingly troubled country's social or political destiny. For
him, as for Karl Barth, the title of Zora Neale Hurston's novel
most pointedly applied: "Their Eyes Were Watching God." Yet,
as noted, exactly two days after Hitler took office Bonhoeffer was
challenging the notion of a "Führer" in a radio address — the
start, it can be said, of a new life for him, a politically engaged

one that would have obvious consequences for him not only as a German but as a Christian and a theologian as well. For a Lutheran from a prominent family to question state authority, and do so publicly, was no small step. In a way he was also questioning religious authority. His plea to his brother ministers that they "confess," that they, in fact, make such a posture of contrition the contemporary hallmark of their faith, that they be members of a confessing faith rather than German Lutherans, was a radical intervention, and set him very much apart: the great majority of his colleagues signed up with Hitler, and even, as noted, wore the Nazi brown shirt at certain meetings.

In two respects, then, Bonhoeffer was breaking with his earlier interests and manner of thinking. He was increasingly concerned with the here and now and he was openly at odds with his own government and his church's relationship to it. Moreover, he became at this time very much a "pacifist." He began to regard war as not only inhumane and destructive but, in the religious sense of the word, profane: a blasphemous act on the part of national leaders and their cohorts. He even wanted to go visit Gandhi, to live in his ashram for a while, to learn from him — one more break with the conservative, Lutheran, German heritage that was initially very much at work in his mind.

By the late 1930s a new person had been born — the one many of us know and, understandably, regard as a major theological and spiritual presence, a twentieth-century gift to Christian thought. But this man so welcome to us did not just spring to life as we know him now. Nor did he come to be the person he became out of an essentially philosophical or theological evolution: Emerson's "thinking man" choosing this or that path during a continuing journey of the self, fueled by its capacity for independent inwardness. This was a man once privileged, admired, and lucky who had now become embattled and lonely, and, in no time, his career and then his very life were in jeopardy. He could not teach in a university or be a pastor in a church. He was under constant investigation. Only his family's high position and many connections spared him (for a while) arrest and worse. Even before the outbreak of war his friends abroad kept worrying about him, wanting to rescue him. And his friends at home, his really close comrades, were more and more part of an opposition fast becoming an underground. Nor, it need be repeatedly said, was any of this turn of events necessary: all Bonhoeffer had to do was keep his strong reservations about the Nazis to himself and his close associates. Instead, he became a public opponent of his nation's leaders, of his church as it accommodated itself to those leaders, and of the policies his government was pursuing: rearmament and the pursuit of land through the threat of war.

Under such circumstances Bonhoeffer turned not to an abstract, distant God, not to his Lutheran past (in hope of redeeming it), not to the intellectual tradition of the Enlightenment, or indeed, to the fashionable thinking that had figured so prominently in the Berlin of the 1920s. He turned rather to Jesus Christ, to His concrete experiences, to His speeches, His parables, His admonitions, suggestions, interpretations, to His declared views as they emerged in the course of His teaching and healing, and, not least, to His life as He chose to live it. A promising theologian became an endangered outcast. It is as if he leapt across nineteen centuries, trying to put himself in the company of Jesus and His chosen fellow pilgrims, a band of humble followers who took their own risks by choosing to stand with Him. Such a leap meant forsaking (even taking on) church and state; and such a leap prompted a distinctive moral and spiritual life. The point now was not to argue or urge reforms or even refuse allegiance to state and church, but to take the most radical of steps, to overthrow an established order of things, a government very much in control, with a church very much its professed ally.

Bonhoeffer's spirituality was not that of a contemporary Christian struggling to find his or her bearings within the church — a Thomas Merton, say, or a Flannery O'Connor. Nor was he a one-time agnostic who had received the miracle of faith — a Simone Weil, an Edith Stein. If, as the saying puts it, "history makes the man," or at least certain persons, who bring a readiness to be deeply affected by a particular historical moment, then it was "the times" that turned young Bonhoeffer, the devout Lutheran communicant, the talented theological student and scholar who saw God's distance from us as a given, a hard and inevitable barrier, and, not least, the politically removed or indifferent German with weightier things (it could perhaps have been said in, say, 1930) on his mind, into someone "scorned and rebuked," an outlaw of a nation once very much his. Bonhoeffer's Christianity became that of the early years of the religion, before it became institutionalized; indeed, his faith during the decisive last decade of his life was comparable to that of an apostle to a Jesus very much still on earth, and very much living on the edge, if not in constant and dire danger. He talks modestly of "discipleship," but he has in mind the apostles before they became such — quite ordinary folk enormously taken by Jesus the man of compelling moral condition who seemed strangely adrift, solitary, and, increasingly, a considerable thorn in the side of all established religious and political authority.

To be sure, the history that beckoned others of Bonhoeffer's intellectual standing or higher (the psychoanalyst Carl Jung, the philosopher Martin Heidegger, the literary critic Paul de Man, the poet Ezra Pound) brought them right through the welcoming doors of Nazism, of Fascism. To the end of his life Heidegger was an unrepentant Nazi, this hero of "existentialism" who preached loftily to us of "authenticity" and who fell like a fool for Hitler and his lying, murderous hoodlums. Jung equivocated, explained and explained again (hoping to explain away) his dalliance with unprecedented darkness. Paul de Man tried to conceal his Nazi affiliation and was found out only posthumously. Pound found in "insanity" an escape from treason, his foul mouth quite a lesson for those of us who preach "the humanities" and "poetry" as an answer to callousness and brutishness of mind and heart. Meanwhile a young pastor took Jesus seriously enough to try to emulate him and was given by fate a chance to do so more closely than anyone would dare to believe possible.

There were signs, no question, that Bonhoeffer had it in him to stand tall against the conformist pressures of the most totalitarian society the world had ever seen. In the summer of 1931 he went to Bonn to hear Karl Barth, spent three weeks hearing him lecture, and was reported to have quoted Luther in one class —

his observation that "the curses of the godless sometimes sound better in God's ear than the hallelujahs of the pious." *There,* the both of them could agree, might be an element in the Lord's train of thought that they could detect and uphold quite distinctly as His. Which of the "godless" might the Lord have enjoyed hearing — Freud, perhaps? In his adamantly skeptical *Future of an Illusion,* Freud made clear his conviction that we use the notion of God to tell of our own needs, desires, and fears: faith as the self writ large. Such an observation, of course, tells us about Freud as well — the psychoanalyst as a continual doubter, in and out of the office. Even as Barth and Bonhoeffer had no wish to conceal their originality and, in time, their joint wish to defy the pious ones now considering themselves proudly, yes, Nazi-sanctioned ministers, the two might not have been surprised if the God whose hunger and thirst, whose own kind of seeking life they had portrayed found a certain pleasure in the rough and ready, polemical talk of the "godless" Freud, who (in the sorting that took place during the 1930s in Germany and in Austria) ended up going into exile, even as his sisters were sent to concentration camps and killed. If the Nazis burnt Freud's books, he did indeed deserve a moment's grateful attention from the Lord whom Barth and Bonhoeffer very much in their humanity were calling to their side.

Indeed, by the end of his life Bonhoeffer was even having grave misgivings about churches, their purpose as supposed instruments of God's message. In an "outline for a book," written in the summer of 1944, he insists that "the church is the church only when it exists for others." Then, lest such an observation be regarded as all too vaporous, he adds: "To make a start, it should give away all its property to those in need."

We are, with that, in the topsy-turvy world of Someone who long ago confounded the "principalities and powers" of his time — as in "the last shall be first, the first last." We are, really, in a pre-church time, and we are in serious connection with an anti-institutional way of seeing things. It took centuries for Christ's life and His words to be brought under control, shed of their radical challenge to those who are owners, leaders, big-shots of various kinds. Bonhoeffer's letters and other writings, at this point (he had less than a year to live) bring him in company with Tolstoy as he contemplated his own kind in *Confession* and called upon a dramatic leveling in the name of faith; or with Silone's *Bread and Wine,* in which the dearly lovable and decent teacher, Don Benedetto, wonders what it is that happens to us as we grow older. Addressing his one-time pupils, now in their thirties, Bonhoeffer's age when he kept his prison diary, Benedetto remembers "something vital and personal" in the children he knew, who only a few years later "already look like cynical and bored men." His heart aches with such knowledge; he yearns for another outcome, and not only for the sake of those former students, but on behalf of all of us: an idealism of action as our only chance to affirm values which, otherwise, become the driest, most reflexic of pieties. But these "grown" men, in the cool, direct, matter-of-fact language of their "maturity" tell him this: "At school you dream, in life you have to adapt yourself. That is the reality. You never become what you would like to become."

No wonder Bonhoeffer in prison had grave doubts about modern psychology as well as contemporary churches — all of them. "Reality," "adapt" — these are the buzz words of today's bourgeois life, as he well knew, and he had taken them on with a vengeance in the years that preceded his imprisonment, hence its occurrence. How well I remember in this regard a professor at Union Theological Seminary, David Roberts, speaking of Bonhoeffer retrospectively in the middle 1950s. I was a medical student auditing a seminar of his, and he dared to ask us what we would have advised Bonhoeffer to "do" in 1938 as he debated the big question: to stay on the American side of the Atlantic, or cross it in order to resist wrong — and to do so when that wrong was becoming the biggest and most implacably consuming (and, it seemed, mightiest) wrong in all history? It was, naturally, easy for us then to slap Bonhoeffer vigorously on the back, applaud him heartily, sing his moral praises. And yet, Professor Roberts reminded us, he was likely headed for an awful, inglorious, and quick death. What would he "really" accomplish? Why was he putting himself in such danger? At the time I didn't know what the Niebuhrs later told me, that lots of people at Union and others elsewhere were asking such questions and thinking along such lines.

Those questions are, alas, not only rhetorical or a sardonic reminder of the manner in which the dignity and usefulness of psychoanalytic psychiatry can (has) become quite something else, a means for many of us to think of *ourselves* all too thoroughly. And once we are headed in that direction, the demands of God must fade into a dominant secular landscape. Moral scruples, the spiritual reality of Christ's exhortations and warnings, yield to another kind of reality, that of the body's one and only chance on this planet, that of the mind's wish to hang around forever. Hence the reality of being "realistic." "The unconscious is time-less," Anna Freud once remarked, her way of observing our rock-bottom refusal to acknowledge death as our destiny. And so we live at all costs, and that being the case, our values and prin-ciples are in constant jeopardy: Will adherence to them threaten the kind of being we treasure most? In Rilke's words, "survival is all."

Bonhoeffer took the measure of that secular mode of thought (it is embraced today by many in the name of religion) most fa-mously, in the last days of his imprisonment, when he scorned the growing emphasis on psychology and existentialist philosophy of his fellow clergymen and their parishioners. But even in 1933, in his lectures, he was troubled by the present-day temptations in the way of faith: the awareness we have, courtesy of science and social science, and how such a modern consciousness can make a mockery of religion, of biblical passages, of a received tradition of assertion, of the practice of conviction. True, Barth had said "enough." He had asked his students and readers to fix their at-tention on God, had ridiculed the frantic efforts of the churches (even the Catholic Church) to catch up, so to speak, with the modern mind, as "pastoral psychology," or the "historical Jesus," or, yes, the "social gospel." Bonhoeffer did not denounce such ef-forts per se; rather, he saw the idolatrous waters which such ships tried to navigate, with ultimate lack of success.

How then to be a believing Christian today — without, that

is, digging in one's heels, returning to an orthodoxy that angrily turns its back on all the secular mind has accomplished? Kierkegaard had a suggestion, and Bonhoeffer studied him closely: the "resignation" of Abraham becomes ours; one believes, no matter one's doubt. But how does that belief become more than a proclaimed clever trick of the mind? Kierkegaard was at pains to illustrate that kind of belief in his rendered version of Abraham's willingness to sacrifice his son Isaac to the Lord's test of such faith (in *Fear and Trembling*). In that gripping spiritual drama is to be found the fullest, gravest challenge to our twentieth-century sensibility: a father will yield his son to the Lord. Reading of it today one shudders, shakes one's head in thorough disbelief. Indeed, such a story almost ludicrously challenges our psychological or sociological thinking: send the father to a doctor, or help families such as this out of their superstitious ignorance, or smile at the theologian who must, finally, be kidding (himself, if not us, clever jester and terrorist that he is).

I go into the above matter here because I believe that the very heart of Bonhoeffer's "sacrifice" (of himself, not his son — but one must think of the love his fiancée and friends felt for him, which he is forsaking out of a felt spiritual imperative) has to be seen as not only a brave civil dissent (though it is that too) but a Christian one — "Christ the center," as the phrase goes, and in this case, the center of a person's willful readiness to resist an all-powerful totalitarian state, no matter the consequence. Such a stand was, needless to say, not the only one possible. Others, with equal tenacity and honor, went to their deaths resisting Hitler out of different reasons of mind and heart, maybe among those others Bonhoeffer's own brother Klaus and his two brothers-in-law. But Dietrich Bonhoeffer had made clear his own spiritual rationale, a way of seeing things that demanded, over the long haul, a witness that had to go beyond prayer, whether in church or through such "outlets" as writing or teaching.

How ironic, then, that in 1952, seven years after Bonhoeffer's death, upon the publication of his prison diaries and correspondence, Karl Barth should describe him as an "impulsive visionary thinker." For years Bonhoeffer waited and wondered what to do,

how to behave; he even withdrew from the scene (Germany),
no doubt in the very "fear and trembling" Kierkegaard knew
to emphasize. Today some of us might all too quickly, in our
imagination, where moral challenges are never tested, jump on
yet another bandwagon, make our (hollow) pledges. This, too, I
would have done: faced Satan down. But the distance between
such an avowal and the deed is huge — scary to contemplate
as an actual, imminent possibility, never mind to travel. Hence
Kierkegaard's phrase "the teleological suspension of the ethical."
Who in one's right mind (*our* viewpoint!) would give up a son
as Abraham was (again, reluctantly and fearfully) ready to do?
When Bonhoeffer the avowed pacifist, the sincere Lutheran, decided to take part in an attempt to kill Hitler, take part in a direct
challenge to the German state, he was not sitting in an armchair
or at a writing desk or in a classroom making a choice that would
earn the ready applause of others, similarly situated. He was, like
Abraham, *in res medias*. And far from being "impulsive," he had
prepared himself inwardly a long time for such an awesome challenge and responsibility: a moment of Christian testing worthy of
Kierkegaard, of the Bible itself.

No wonder, in his last year or two as a prisoner, Bonhoeffer
turned to fiction and poetry. He worked at a novel; he wrote letters; he wrote short stories; he constructed a play. And he left
us with poems that sing both mournfully and joyfully, their con-
cise, dense language his endeavor to say so very much in the
pointed way of verse. Such writing signals a realization on his
part that he had crossed a bridge, moved beyond the erudite,
contentious paradigms and expositions and disputations of theology. His was, by then, a theology of the individual as Christ's
witness, of a "religionless" Christianity, of Jesus as a constant
spiritual teacher, immensely heartening yet terribly unnerving and
demanding, rather than a distant God worshiped on Sundays in
church or acknowledged piously in prayers. He was in prison,
and as the days turned to months, and he moved from prison
to prison, ever more ominously, it became clear to him that he
might continue to hope, but that, really, he could only hope
against hope. And so the stories, the lyrical inwardness shared,

the brief messages and longer forays into plots, characters, dramatic scenes, dialogue: a world of words meant to tell of concrete deeds done, events that transpired.

He was a novice, of course. He lacked the "craft" to leave us with "great" fiction or poetry. But he was revealing to us a turn of mind, of heart. And his letters are in the tradition, surely, of Paul's or, nearer to our place and time, Dr. King's sent from a jail in Birmingham, Alabama. The point was to tell stories, hearken back to his own experiences, render narratively their complexity, so that he (as his own reader) and others might understand, by indirection, what had been transpiring during this terrible travail — a theology grounded in the psalms of the Old Testament, the parables of Jesus the man, the wayfarer.

For many of us Dietrich Bonhoeffer belongs in the company of martyrs, men and women who have stood up, unto death, for their high moral and spiritual principles. Unlike others (we must keep remembering) who were forcibly rounded up and sent to death camps, he had every chance to avoid that fate. He might even have done so. He might have lived a secure, comfortable life and been highly regarded as one of the first Germans to see Hitler for what he was, to denounce him publicly, to lose his pastoral and professional positions — and only then, say, go into exile, as Barth and Tillich and thousands of other distinguished Germans did. Instead, he turned aside opportunity after opportunity to go abroad and to stay abroad in order to fulfill what he passionately believed to be his calling as a German, a Christian, one whose family had been treated so well over the generations by a nation that now in return required from its moral leaders, so he believed, everything they had to give. He did give everything, even as his Lord and Master had over nineteen hundred years earlier.

The psychology of the martyr is the psychology of will, of a decision made and its consequences be damned. In this age of determinisms, emotional and social and historical and economic, there is little room for will in the vocabulary we summon when we try to understand human affairs. Sometimes first things get overlooked in our rush for the less obvious. Erik Erikson, talking about psychoanalysis and his study of Luther once observed:

"Willfulness often is regarded as a secondary trait — we rush to explain the reasons for it. I believe some people have learned to be willful about their beliefs — their willfulness is a big part of them, and it is summoned by them in pursuit of whatever it is they want to uphold. Perhaps that is what 'leadership' is all about — the person who won't take no for an answer: he believes something and he'll do everything it takes to get across what it is he believes, and why. Others with the same outlook — well, they aren't as committed to their ideals, or they don't know how to stick to their guns, live up to their word, 'so help me God,' as it's put."

Bonhoeffer's willfulness was not unlike that of two other pilgrims of his time: Edith Stein, who was born in Breslau like him and lived during his first six years when he too lived in that city; and Simone Weil, who also died in her thirties and who like him was ready to give her all — as a fighter in the French resistance — though she would die, instead, of tuberculosis two years before he did. I mention those two Jewish-born intellectuals because I believe their attitudes, in certain respects, help us understand what Bonhoeffer was trying to accomplish. Stein became a distinguished philosopher; she worked closely with Edmund Husserl and helped extend the reach of phenomenological philosophy and psychology — an emphasis on the individual in all his or her complexity, particularity, and ambiguity. He hungered after each person's distinct soulfulness and tried to do justice to such a vision in the language of the academy, no mean task, and especially so these days when the social sciences with their sweeping categorizations and generalizations threaten to herd us all into thoroughly unqualified formulations, the *this* or *that* of our theorists, who have their own ways of running roughshod over the varieties of human experience. In time, Stein's powerfully gifted mind sought an inward expressiveness of its very own, and so in the Christianity of the Catholic Church she found at once an intellectual and personal home. Her conversion and her decision to become a nun were steps of affirmation for her. But they were nonetheless painful, given the anti-Semitism endemic to Europe at the time, a hatred to which she had no desire to surrender through self-hatred, through what could be interpreted as an escape. Her head held high, indeed, her love for her Jewish people intact, she nevertheless traveled down a road she resolutely decided to be a correct one for her — an unyielding idiosyncratic insistence on her part, one not unlike Bonhoeffer's. Where others shirked going, those two asserted as the only destination they would, could, should choose for themselves. They both died at the hands of the Nazis within a year of one another, she amid the unspeakable degradation of a concentration camp, a place of mass murder; he in the relatively more comfortable conditions (there were camps and camps) granted to certain prisoners whose privileges, ironically, had become a sign of the perplexity they as individuals inspired in their pitiably abased captors: what in the world do we *make* of Bonhoeffer, so very distinguished and yet willing to put himself at such a radical, judgmental remove from those who hold his nation's power?

As for Simone Weil, she spent her all too brief life (she died at thirty-four) studying "power" as it shapes the lives of various men and women and nations and becomes worked into the values of certain writers or cultures. She too gradually came into a religiously awake sensibility and as a consequence experienced a growing loneliness matched by the incomprehensibility others felt with respect to her interests, preferences, and opinions. Like Bonhoeffer she sought Christ in Harlem's churches, not out of any faddish indulgence or condescension but as an aspect of her own moral and spiritual awareness. Here is where the prophetic tradition of Isaiah and Jeremiah and Amos and Micah and Jesus of Nazareth would have us be — in solidarity with outsiders and, further, *as* (would-be) outsiders, each of us in our particular and various ways. Weil was regarded as "mad" for abandoning an academic or literary or political life for that of a factory worker, a farm worker, a supplicant of the Lord in a Harlem church, and, she hoped in vain, a resistance fighter against the Nazis on her native French turf. She, too, chose to leave the security of Manhattan — her parents lived not far from Union Theological Seminary — for a return to Europe. Bonhoeffer had heads astir all along as he relinquished not only voluntarily but out of felt

moral desperation all sorts of options, prerogatives and immu-
nities in favor of his outsider's position, that of a "criminal" as
defined by a sovereign nation trying to become the center of yet
another Roman empire.

To stand outside the gates of money and power and rank and
approved success and applause, to be regarded as irregular or odd
or "sick" or, that final exile, as a traitor — such an outcome, in
this era, carries its own special burdens and demands: the disap-
proval, if not derision, of colleagues, neighbors, the larger world
of commentators who meticulously fall in line with reigning authority, but perhaps most devastating of all, the sense of oneself
that is left in one's mind at the end of a day. What *am* I trying
to do — and is this, after all, not only futile, but evidence that
I have somehow gone astray? In that regard, those of us who
have been granted the right to decide what is "normal" or "ab-
normal" ought be made nervous, indeed, by the likes of a Weil
or a Bonhoeffer, as was the case, I suspect, even in 1939, when
the psychiatric manner of thinking held less sway than is now
the case.

Arguably, all Christian theology is an effort to understand the
meaning of an individual quite provocatively eccentric, who was
put to His death, no less, as an utterly reprehensible criminal.
As if theologians haven't always had enough on their hands: to
make sense of someone whose words and deeds, speeches and
proclaimed ideas, stories and ways of being amounted (in the
judgment of just about everyone important and educated) to social and religious craziness. Now, in this century, those same
scholars have been required to take on an individual who had
the whole (conventional) world in his hands and seemed driven
to give it up in favor of an increasingly certain confinement and
extinction. "There was a lot of head scratching," Professor David
Roberts kept saying to us at Union Theological Seminary, and
therein lies an important aspect, indeed, of Dietrich Bonhoeffer's
legacy. He became a modern martyr precisely because he dared
to risk just such medical misgivings, just such ostracism, refusal,
and condemnation, the highfalutin head-shaking at faculty clubs,
the serious frowns at psychiatric seminars, perhaps even harder

for him to endure than the actions of the Nazi police and judges, those flunkies of totalitarianism. Hence the way he strikes out in his later correspondence against his own (supposed) kind, the "psychotherapists" and "existential philosophers."

The heart of Bonhoeffer's spiritual legacy to us is not to be found in his words, his books, but in the way he spent his time on this earth, in his decision to live as if the Lord were a neighbor and friend, a constant source of courage and inspiration, a presence amid travail and joy alike, a reminder of love's obligations and affirmations and also of death's decisive meaning (how we die as a measure of how we have lived, of who we are). Bonhoeffer abandoned cleverness with language, brilliance at abstract formulation; he forsook denominational argument, oaths and pledges and avowals. In the end he reached out to all of us who crave, in hunger and in thirst, God's grace. And, one believes, unwittingly (how can it be otherwise?), unself-consciously, he became its witness, its recipient. His spiritual gift to us, especially, is his life. The principles he avowed and discussed in his writings gain their authority from the manner in which he conducted that life.

As two thousand years of Christianity come to an end, the witness of Dietrich Bonhoeffer, in all its near storybook drama, reminds us that if evil can be, as Hannah Arendt observed, "banal" in its everyday enactment, then good can be surprising in its occurrence, tenacious in its vitality, no matter the overwhelming odds against its survival. In the end, Hitler showed us a "heart of darkness," beating all too horribly fast, not in a distant jungle but right in our very midst, in our living rooms and our classrooms and, alas, even our churches and seminaries. It is just such a near-at-hand truth that Dietrich Bonhoeffer grasped right away, when others closed their eyes or calculated cravenly their immediate prospects. But he went that one further step; he remembered Jesus not intellectually or theologically or historically, but as our intimate teacher He meant Himself to be, the One who holds us to a certain moral and spiritual mark, and won't let go of us — if, that is, we are truly prepared, at whatever risk, to stay engaged with Him, to follow in His footsteps.

This is the biggest "if" possible, and an "if" whose consequences, at the least, include the head-shaking of others, not to mention rejection, displacement, and worse. "I come to bring you not peace, but the sword," said this Visitor of visitors, signifying the severe disruption that a serious-minded faith, resolutely worked into a life, can prompt in someone who has signed up with such an Arrival, as it were: the Lord, no less, *here,* in our one and only mortal time of it, ready to take our hand and — no matter the turmoil, the hurt, and even the deathly pain — lead us to His *there.*

1

Jesus Christ and the Essence of Christianity

In 1928, after completing his first dissertation, Bonhoeffer accepted a position as curate to a German-speaking Lutheran congregation in Barcelona, Spain. There he delivered this address on December 11, 1928. This translation is reprinted from Geffrey B. Kelly and F. Burton Nelson, eds., A Testament to Freedom: The Essential Writings of Dietrich Bonhoeffer *(New York: HarperCollins, 1990).*

Whether in our time Christ can still occupy a place where we make decisions on the deepest matters known to us, over our own life and over the life of our people, that is the question which we will consider today. Whether or not the Spirit of Christ has anything final, definitive, and decisive to say to us, that is what we want to speak about. We all know that Christ has, in effect, been eliminated from our lives. Of course, we build him a temple, but we live in our own houses. Christ has become a matter of the church or, rather, of the churchiness of a group, not a matter of life. Religion plays for the psyche of the nineteenth and twentieth centuries the role of the so-called Sunday room into which one gladly withdraws for a couple of hours but only to get back to one's place of work immediately afterward. However, one thing is clear: we understand Christ only if we commit ourselves to him in a stark "Either-Or." He did not go to the cross to ornament and

43

embellish our life. If we wish to have him, then he demands the right to say something decisive about our entire life. We do not understand him if we arrange for him only a small compartment in our spiritual life. Rather, we understand our spiritual life only if we then orientate it to him alone or give him a flat "No." However, there are persons who would not even bother to take Christ seriously in the demand he makes on us by his question: will you follow me wholeheartedly or not at all? Such persons had better not mix their own cause with the Christian one. That separation would only help the Christian cause since they no longer have anything in common with Christ. The religion of Christ is not a tidbit after one's bread; on the contrary, it is bread or it is nothing. People should at least understand and concede this if they call themselves Christian.

Many attempts have been made to eliminate Christ from the present life of the spirit. Indeed, what is so seductive about these attempts is that it appears as if Christ would be promoted, for the first time, to his proper place, that is, a place worthy of him. One admires Christ according to aesthetic categories as an aesthetic genius, calls him the greatest ethicist; one admires his going to his death as a heroic sacrifice for his ideas. Only one thing one doesn't do: one doesn't take him seriously. That is, one doesn't bring the center of his or her own life into contact with the claim of Christ to speak the revelation of God and to be that revelation. One maintains a distance between himself or herself and the word of Christ, and allows no serious encounter to take place. I can doubtless live with or without Jesus as a religious genius, as an ethicist, as a gentlemen — just as, after all, I can also live without Plato and Kant — all that has only relative meaning. Should, however, there be something in Christ that claims my life entirely with the full seriousness that here God himself speaks and if the word of God once became present only in Christ, then Christ has not only relative but absolute, urgent significance for me. To be sure, I still have the free choice of "yes" or "no," but in the end I am indifferent to such a choice. Understanding Christ means taking Christ seriously. Understanding this claim means taking seriously his absolute claim on our commitment.

And it is now of importance for us to clarify the seriousness of this matter and to extricate Christ from the secularization process in which he has been incorporated since the Enlightenment, and finally, to show that even in our days the question to which Christ gives an answer is so completely crucial that here is where the Spirit of Christ justly makes his claim. Thus is raised our first and main question about the essence of the Christian message, the essence of Christianity.

There is pronounced, therefore, a fundamental criticism against the most grandiose of all human attempts to approach the divine — against the church. Christianity contains a seed of animosity to the church since we wish to base a demand on God on our devotion to Christ and church. Thereby, we again fully misunderstand the Christian idea and fail in our efforts. Yet Christianity needs the church. That is the paradox. And here lies the enormous responsibility the church has to bear.

Ethics and religion lie in the direction of humans toward God. Christ, however, speaks alone, entirely alone, of the direction of God to people; not of the human way to God but of the way of God to humans. Therefore, it is likewise completely perverse to seek a new morality in Christianity. Factually speaking, Christ has given scarcely any ethical prescriptions that were not to be found already with the contemporary Jewish rabbis or in pagan literature. The essence of Christianity lies in the message of the sovereign God to whom alone belongs glory over all the world. It is the message of the eternally other, the one who is far above the world, yet who from the depth of his being has mercy on the person who gives glory to him alone. He is the one who goes on the way to people in order to seek vessels of his glory where the human person is no longer anything, where he becomes silent, where he gives way to God alone.

Here the light of eternity shines down on those who are ever neglected, insignificant, weak, ignoble, unknown, inferior, opposed, despised; here it radiates over the houses of prostitutes and tax collectors. Here the light of eternity has been cast on the toiling, struggling, and sinning masses. The word of grace spreads across the stale sultriness of the big cities, but it halts before the houses of the satisfied, the knowledgeable, and the "haves" of this world in a spiritual sense. It speaks over the death of individuals and peoples its everlasting word: I have loved you from eternity; remain with me; thus will you live. Christianity preaches the unending worth of the apparently worthless and the unending worthlessness of what is apparently so valuable. The weak shall be made strong through God and the dying shall live.

Has Christianity only pointed to another religion, a new idea of culture? Has it shown only a human way to God that had not yet been used? No; the Christian idea is the way of God to people and has as the visible objectification of this, the cross. Here lies the point at which we are accustomed to turn away shaking our heads about the Christian cause. The cross was probably first set at the center of the Christian message by Paul. Jesus has said nothing about this. And yet the correct meaning of the cross of Christ is nothing else than radical development of the concept of God held by Jesus himself. It is, so to speak, the historically visible form which this concept of God has assumed. God comes to people who have nothing but room for God — and this hollow space, this emptiness in people is called in Christian speech, faith. This means that in Jesus of Nazareth, his revealer, God inclines to the sinner; Jesus seeks the companionship of the sinner, goes after him or her in boundless love. He wants to be where a human person is no longer anything. The meaning of the life of Jesus is the demonstration of this divine will for sinners, for those who are unworthy. Where Jesus is, there is the love of God. However, the demonstration becomes complete, not when Jesus or God's love exists where the human person lives in sin and misery, but only when Jesus also takes upon himself the fate that hangs over every life, namely, death. That is when Jesus who is God's love really dies. Only then can a person be certain that God's love accompanies and leads him or her through death. The death of Jesus on the cross of criminals, however, shows that the divine love even finds its way to the death of the criminal. And when Jesus dies on the cross with the cry, "My God why have you abandoned me" (Mark 15:34), does this mean that God's eternal will to love does not abandon people even when in the experience of being abandoned by God they are plunged into despair? Jesus dies really despairing of his work, of God, but that of all things just signifies the culmination of his message that God so loves people that he takes death upon himself for their sake as proof of his own will to love. And, only because in the humiliation on the cross Jesus demonstrates his own and God's love for the world, resurrection follows after death. Death cannot restrain love. "Love is stronger than death" (Song of Songs 8:6).

That is the meaning of Good Friday and Easter Sunday: the way of God to people leads back to God. In this way Jesus' own concept of God is joined together with Paul's interpretation of the cross. Thus the cross becomes the central and paradoxical symbol of the Christian message. A king who goes to the cross must be the king of a wonderful kingdom. Only the one who understands the deep paradox of the idea of the cross can understand the entire meaning of the word of Jesus: my kingdom is not of this world. Jesus had to reject the king's crown that was offered him, had to deny the idea of the Roman imperium which would have been a temptation for him at every turn, if he were to remain true to his idea of God which led him to the cross.

The answer to another pressing question follows from this interpretation of the cross of Christ: what are we to think of other religions? Are they as nothing compared to Christianity? We answer that the Christian religion as religion is not of God. It is rather another example of a human way to God, like the Buddhist and others, too, though of course, these are of a different nature. Christ is not the bringer of a new religion, but rather the one who brings God. Therefore, as an impossible way from the human to God, the Christian religion stands with other religions. The Christian can never pride himself on his Christianity, for it remains human, all too human. He lives, however, by the grace of God, which comes to people and comes to every person who opens his or her heart to it and learns to understand it in the cross of Christ. And, therefore, the gift of Christ is not the Christian religion, but the grace and love of God which culminate in the cross.

2

Christ the Center

In the spring of 1933 Adolf Hitler became chancellor of Germany with dictatorial powers. That summer, at the University of Berlin, Bonhoeffer delivered a series of lectures on christology, later published as Christ the Center. *The following selection comes from the introduction to that work.*

Teaching about Christ begins in silence. "Be silent, for that is the absolute" (Kierkegaard). This has nothing to do with mystical silence which, in its absence of words, is, nevertheless, the soul secretly chattering away to itself. The church's silence is silence before the Word. In proclaiming the Word, the church must fall silent before the inexpressible: Let what cannot be spoken be worshiped in silence (Cyril of Alexandria). The spoken Word is the inexpressible: that which cannot be spoken is the Word. It must be spoken, it is the great battle cry of the church (Luther). The church utters it in the world, yet it still remains the inexpressible. To speak of Christ means to keep silent; to be silent about Christ means to speak. The proclamation of Christ is the church speaking from a proper silence.

We are concerned here with the meaning of this proclamation. Its content is revealed only in the proclamation itself. To speak of Christ, then, will be to speak within the context of the silence of the church. We must study christology in the humble silence of the worshiping community. Prayer is to be silent and to cry out at the same time, before God in the presence of his Word. We have come together as a community to study Christ,

God's Word. We have not met in church, but in the lecture room. We have academic work to do....

Let us return to the beginning. To what extent is the christological question the central question of scholarship? It has this significance inasmuch as it alone has put the question of transcendence in the form of the question of existence, inasmuch as the ontological question has here been put as the question of the being of a person, the person Jesus Christ. The old Logos is judged by the transcendence of the person of Christ and learns to understand it correctly within its necessary limitations. As logology, christology alone makes scholarship possible. But this is to touch only on the formal side.

The matter of content is more important. Human reason is strained to the limit by the question "Who?" What happens when the Anti-Logos raises his claim? Man annihilates the "Who?" with whom he is confronted. "Who are you?" asks Pilate. Jesus is silent. Man cannot wait for the dangerous answer. The Logos cannot endure the Anti-Logos. It knows that one of them must die. So it kills the person of whom it has asked. Because the human Logos does not want to die, the Logos of God, who would be the death of it, must die so that it can live on with its unanswered questions of existence and transcendence. The Logos of God incarnate must be crucified by man's Logos. The one who compelled the dangerous question is killed, the question dies with him.

But what happens if this Counter-Word, though killed, rises living and victorious from the dead as the ultimate Word of God? If he sets himself up before his murderers? If the Crucified shows himself as the Risen One? Here the question "Who are you?" reaches its sharpest climax. Here it stands vividly forever over, around, and in man, as question and as answer. Man can struggle against the Incarnate, but in the face of the Risen One he is powerless. Now he is himself the one who is judged and killed. The question is reversed and rebounds on the human Logos. "Who are you, to ask thus?" "Are you truly there, to ask thus?" "Who are you, who can still only inquire after me when I restore you, justify you, and give you my grace?"

The christological question "Who?" is finally formulated only where this reversed question is also heard. The mere fact that man for his part can be questioned like this shows who it is who asks. Only God can ask like this. A man cannot put these questions to his fellow. In that case, the only question which can be returned is "Who are you?" Questions of "fact," the question "How?" have lost all meaning.

What can that mean in particular? Even today the Unknown One meets men on the road in such a way that they can only ask the question "Who are you?" however often they try to parry it. They must come to grips with him. We must also come to grips with Goethe and Socrates. On this our education and our ethos depend. But on our coming to grips with Christ depend life and death, salvation and damnation. This cannot be appreciated from outside. But in the church it is the principle on which everything rests. "And there is salvation in no one else" (Acts 4:12). The cause of the encounter with Jesus is not the same as that of the encounter with Socrates and Goethe. It is impossible to avoid the person of Jesus because he is alive. If need be, Goethe can be avoided because he is dead. Thousands of attempts have been made to resist or to avoid meeting Jesus.

For the working-class world, Christ seems to be settled with the church and bourgeois society. There is no longer any reason why the worker should encounter Jesus Christ. The church is all one with the fossilized sanctions of the capitalist system. But at this very point, the working class may distinguish between Jesus and his church; *he* is not the guilty party. Up with Jesus, down with the church. Here Jesus can become the idealist, the socialist. What does it mean when, in his world of suspicion and distrust, the worker says, "Jesus was a good man"? It means that there is no need to distrust *him*. The worker does not say "Jesus is God." But when he says "Jesus was a good man" he is at any rate saying more than when the bourgeois says, "Jesus is God." God for him is something which belongs to the church. But Jesus can be present on the factory floor as the socialist, in politics as the idealist, in the workers' own world as the good man. He fights in their ranks against the enemy, capitalism. Who are you? Are you our brother and Lord? Is the question merely evaded here? Or do they, in their own way, put it seriously?

Dostoievsky portrayed the figure of Christ in the splendor of Russian culture in his novel *The Idiot*. The idiot does not keep himself apart, but clumsily causes offense everywhere. He has nothing to do with the great ones, but with the children. He is mocked and he is loved. He is the fool and he is the wise man. He endures all and he forgives all. He is revolutionary, yet he conforms. He does not want to — but he draws attention to himself simply by being there. Who are you? Idiot or Christ?

One might think of Gerhard Hauptmann's novel, *Der Narr in Christo Emanuel Quint;* or of the description and distortions of Christ written by Wilhelm Gross and Georg Grosz, behind which there lurks the question, "Who are you really?" Christ goes through the ages, questioned anew, missed anew, killed anew.

The theologian makes the same attempt to encounter Jesus or to get round him. Theologians betray him and simulate concern. Christ is always betrayed by the kiss. To want to deal with him always means to fall prostrate with the mockers and to say, "Hail, Rabbi!" In the end, there are only two possibilities of encountering Jesus: either man must die or he kills Jesus.

The question "Who are you?" remains ambiguous. It can be the question of the one who knows that he has been encountered and can hear already the counter-question, "And who are you?" But it can also be the question of the person who, when he asks, means, "How can I deal with you?" In that case, the question is simply a disguised form of the question "How?" The question "Who?" can be put to Jesus only when the counter-question has been heard. In that case it is not man who has dealt with Jesus, but Jesus who has dealt with man. So the question "Who?" is to be spoken only in faith.

As long as the christological question is the question of the human Logos, it remains stuck in the ambivalence of the question "How?" But if it is asked in the act of faith, it has the possibility of putting the question "Who?"

There are two contrasting types of authority: the authority of the office and the authority of the person. The question to the authority of the office is "What are you?" The "What?" concerns the office. The question to the authority of the person is, "Whence do you have this authority?" The answer is, "From you, who acknowledge my authority over you." Both questions can be derived from the question "How?" and can be assigned a place within it. It assumes that, basically, each man is as I am. The presupposition is that the person who is asked can be similar to me in his being. The authorities are merely bearers of the authority of a community, bearers of an office, bearers of a word. They are not the office itself or the word itself. Even the prophets are what they are only as bearers of a word. But what happens if someone appears with the claim that he not only *has* authority but *is* authority; not only *has* a word but *is* the Word? Here our being is invaded by a new being. Here the highest authority in the world so far, the prophet, is at an end. This is no longer a holy man, a reformer, a prophet, but the Son. The question is no longer, "What or whence are you?" The question here concerns revelation itself.

3

The Cost of Discipleship

The Cost of Discipleship, which was published in 1937, was the most radical work of Bonhoeffer to appear during his lifetime. His concern here was not only the idolatrous nature of the Nazi state but the deadly compromises of the so-called German Christians who substituted loyalty to the Reich for obedience to the cross.

COSTLY GRACE

Cheap grace is the deadly enemy of our church. We are fighting today for costly grace.

Cheap grace means grace sold on the market like cheapjacks' wares. The sacraments, the forgiveness of sin, and the consolations of religion are thrown away at cut prices. Grace is represented as the church's inexhaustible treasury, from which she showers blessings with generous hands, without asking questions or fixing limits. Grace without price; grace without cost! The essence of grace, we suppose, is that the account has been paid in advance; and, because it has been paid, everything can be had for nothing. Since the cost was infinite, the possibilities of using and spending it are infinite. What would grace be if it were not cheap?

Cheap grace means grace as a doctrine, a principle, a system. It means forgiveness of sins proclaimed as a general truth, the love of God taught as the Christian "conception" of God. An intellectual assent to that idea is held to be of itself sufficient to secure remission of sins. The church which holds the correct doctrine of grace has, it is supposed, ipso facto a part in that grace. In such a church the world finds a cheap covering for its sins; no contrition is required, still less any real desire to be delivered from sin. Cheap grace therefore amounts to a denial of the living Word of God, in fact, a denial of the Incarnation of the Word of God.

Cheap grace means the justification of sin without the justification of the sinner. Grace alone does everything, they say, and so everything can remain as it was before. . . .

Yet it is imperative for the Christian to achieve renunciation, to practice self-effacement, to distinguish his life from the life of the world. He must let grace be grace indeed, otherwise he will destroy the world's faith in the free gift of grace. Let the Christian rest content with his worldliness and with this renunciation of any higher standard than the world. He is doing it for the sake of the world rather than for the sake of grace. Let him be comforted and rest assured in his possession of this grace — for grace alone does everything. Instead of following Christ, let the Christian enjoy the consolations of his grace! That is what we mean by cheap grace, the grace which amounts to the justification of sin without the justification of the repentant sinner who departs from sin and from whom sin departs. Cheap grace is not the kind of forgiveness of sin which frees us from the toils of sin. Cheap grace is the grace we bestow on ourselves.

Cheap grace is the preaching of forgiveness without requiring repentance, baptism without church discipline, Communion without confession, absolution without personal confession. Cheap grace is grace without discipleship, grace without the cross, grace without Jesus Christ, living and incarnate.

Costly grace is the treasure hidden in the field; for the sake of it a man will gladly go and sell all he has. It is the pearl of great price to buy which the merchant will sell all his goods. It is the kingly rule of Christ, for whose sake a man will pluck out the eye which causes him to stumble; it is the call of Jesus Christ at which the disciple leaves his nets and follows him.

Costly grace is the gospel which must be *sought* again and again, the gift which must be *asked* for, the door at which a man must *knock*.

Such grace is *costly* because it calls us to follow, and it is *grace* because it calls us to follow *Jesus Christ*. It is costly because it costs a man his life, and it is grace because it gives a man the only true life. It is costly because it condemns sin, and grace because it justifies the sinner. Above all, it is *costly* because it cost God the life of his Son: "ye were bought at a price," and what has cost God much cannot be cheap for us. Above all, it is *grace* because God did not reckon his Son too dear a price to pay for our life, but delivered him up for us. Costly grace is the Incarnation of God.

Costly grace is the sanctuary of God; it has to be protected from the world and not thrown to the dogs. It is therefore the living word, the Word of God, which he speaks as it pleases him. Costly grace confronts us as a gracious call to follow Jesus; it comes as a word of forgiveness to the broken spirit and the contrite heart. Grace is costly because it compels a man to submit to the yoke of Christ and follow him; it is grace because Jesus says: "My yoke is easy and my burden is light." ...

It is a fatal misunderstanding of Luther's action to suppose that his rediscovery of the gospel of pure grace offered a general dispensation from obedience to the command of Jesus, or that it was the great discovery of the Reformation that God's forgiving grace automatically conferred upon the world both righteousness and holiness. On the contrary, for Luther the Christian's worldly calling is sanctified only insofar as that calling registers the final, radical protest against the world. Only insofar as the Christian's secular calling is exercised in the following of Jesus does it receive from the gospel new sanction and justification. It was not the justification of sin, but the justification of the sinner that drove Luther from the cloister back into the world. The grace he had received was costly grace. It was grace, for it was like water on parched ground, comfort in tribulation, freedom from the bondage of a self-chosen way, and forgiveness of all his sins. And it was costly, for, so far from dispensing him from good works, it meant that he must take the call to discipleship more seriously than ever before. It was grace because it cost so much, and it cost so much because it was grace. That was the secret of the gospel of the Reformation — the justification of the sinner.

Yet the outcome of the Reformation was the victory, not of Luther's perception of grace in all its purity and costliness, but of the vigilant religious instinct of man for the place where grace is to be obtained at the cheapest price. All that was needed was a subtle and almost imperceptible change of emphasis, and the damage was done. Luther had taught that man cannot stand before God, however religious his works and ways may be, because at bottom he is always seeking his own interests. In the depth of his misery, Luther had grasped by faith the free and unconditional forgiveness of all his sins. That experience taught him that this grace had cost him his very life, and must continue to cost him the same price day by day. So far from dispensing him from discipleship, this grace only made him a more earnest disciple. When he spoke of grace, Luther always implied as a corollary that it cost him his own life, the life which was now for the first time subjected to the absolute obedience of Christ. Only so could he speak of grace. Luther had said that grace alone can save; his followers took up his doctrine and repeated it word for word. But they left out its invariable corollary, the obligation of discipleship. There was no need for Luther always to mention that corollary explicitly for he always spoke as one who had been led by grace to the strictest following of Christ. Judged by the standard of Luther's doctrine, that of his followers was unassailable, and yet their orthodoxy spelled the end and destruction of the Reformation as the revelation on earth of the costly grace of God. The justification of the sinner in the world degenerated into the justification of sin and the world. Costly grace was turned into cheap grace without discipleship. . . .

But do we also realize that this cheap grace has turned back upon us like a boomerang? The price we are having to pay today in the shape of the collapse of the organized church is only the

inevitable consequence of our policy of making grace available
to all at too low a cost. We gave away the word and sacraments wholesale, we baptized, confirmed, and absolved a whole
nation unasked and without condition. Our humanitarian sentiment made us give that which was holy to the scornful and
unbelieving. We poured forth unending streams of grace. But the
call to follow Jesus in the narrow way was hardly ever heard.
Where were those truths which impelled the early church to in-
stitute the catechumenate, which enabled a strict watch to be
kept over the frontier between the church and the world, and af-
forded adequate protection for costly grace? What had happened
to all those warnings of Luther's against preaching the gospel in
such a manner as to make men rest secure in their ungodly living? Was there ever a more terrible or disastrous instance of the
Christianizing of the world than this? What are those three thousands Saxons put to death by Charlemagne compared with the
millions of spiritual corpses in our country today? With us it has
been abundantly proved that the sins of the fathers are visited
upon the children unto the third and fourth generations. Cheap
grace has turned out to be utterly merciless to our Evangelical
Church. . . .

Happy are they who have reached the end of the road we
seek to tread, who are astonished to discover the by no means
self-evident truth that grace is costly just because it is the grace
of God in Jesus Christ. Happy are the simple followers of Jesus
Christ who have been overcome by his grace and are able to sing
the praises of the all-sufficient grace of Christ with humbleness
of heart. Happy are they who, knowing that grace, can live in
the world without being of it, who, by following Jesus Christ, are
so assured of their heavenly citizenship that they are truly free
to live their lives in this world. Happy are they who know that
discipleship simply means the life which springs from grace, and
that grace simply means discipleship. Happy are they who have
become Christians in this sense of the word. For them the word
of grace has proved a fount of mercy.

DISCIPLESHIP AND THE CROSS

And he began to teach them, that the Son of man must suffer many things, and be rejected by the elders, and the chief priests, and the scribes, and be killed, and after three days rise again.... (Mark 8:31)

Here the call to follow is closely connected with Jesus' prediction of his passion. Jesus Christ must suffer and be rejected. This "must" is inherent in the promise of God — the Scripture must be fulfilled. There is a distinction here between suffering and rejection. Had he only suffered, Jesus might still have been applauded as the Messiah. All the sympathy and admiration of the world might have been focused on his passion. It could have been viewed as a tragedy with its own intrinsic value, dignity, and honor. But in the passion Jesus is a rejected Messiah. His rejection robs the passion of its halo of glory. It must be a passion without honor. Suffering and rejection sum up the whole cross of Jesus. To die on the cross means to die despised and rejected of men. Suffering and rejection are laid upon Jesus as a divine necessity, and every attempt to prevent it is the work of the devil, especially when it comes from his own disciples; for it is in fact an attempt to prevent Christ from being Christ. It is Peter, the Rock of the Church, who commits that sin, immediately after he has confessed Jesus as the Messiah and has been appointed to the primacy. That shows how the very notion of a suffering Messiah was a scandal to the church, even in its earliest days. That is not the kind of Lord it wants, and as the church of Christ it does not like to have the law of suffering imposed upon it by its Lord. Peter's protest displays his own unwillingness to suffer, and that means that Satan has gained entry into the church, and is trying to tear it away from the cross of its Lord.

Jesus must therefore make it clear beyond all doubt that the "must" of suffering applies to his disciples no less than to himself. Just as Christ is Christ only in virtue of his suffering and rejection, so the disciple is a disciple only insofar as he shares his

Lord's suffering and rejection and crucifixion. Discipleship means adherence to the person of Jesus, and therefore submission to the law of Christ which is the law of the cross.

Surprisingly enough, when Jesus begins to unfold this inescapable truth to his disciples, he once more sets them free to choose or reject him. "If any man would come after me," he says. For it is not a matter of course, not even among the disciples. Nobody can be forced, nobody can even be expected to come. He says rather "If any man" is prepared to spurn all other offers which come his way in order to follow him. Once again, everything is left for the individual to decide. When the disciples are half-way along the road of discipleship, they come to another crossroad. Once more they are left free to choose for themselves, nothing is expected of them, nothing forced upon them. So crucial is the demand of the present hour that the disciples must be left free to make their own choice before they are told of the law of discipleship.

"If any man would come after me, let him deny himself." The disciple must say to himself the same words Peter said of Christ when he denied him: "I know not this man." Self-denial is never just a series of isolated acts of mortification or asceticism. It is not suicide, for there is an element of self-will even in that. To deny oneself is to be aware only of Christ and no more of self, to see only him who goes before and no more the road which is too hard for us. Once more, all that self-denial can say is: "He leads the way, keep close to him."

" ... and take up his cross." Jesus has graciously prepared the way for this word by speaking first of self-denial. Only when we have become completely oblivious of self are we ready to bear the cross for his sake. If in the end we know only him, if we have ceased to notice the pain of our own cross, we are indeed looking only unto him. If Jesus had not so graciously prepared us for this word, we should have found it unbearable. But by preparing us for it he has enabled us to receive even a word as hard as this as a word of grace. It comes to us in the joy of discipleship and confirms us in it.

To endure the cross is not a tragedy; it is the suffering which is the fruit of an exclusive allegiance to Jesus Christ. When it comes, it is not an accident, but a necessity. It is not the sort of suffering which is inseparable from this mortal life, but the suffering which is an essential part of the specifically Christian life. It is not suffering per se but suffering-and-rejection, and not rejection for any cause or conviction of our own, but rejection for the sake of Christ. If our Christianity has ceased to be serious about discipleship, if we have watered down the gospel into emotional uplift which makes no costly demands and which fails to distinguish between natural and Christian existence, then we cannot help regarding the cross as an ordinary everyday calamity, as one of the trials and tribulations of life. We have then forgotten that the cross means rejection and shame as well as suffering. The Psalmist was lamenting that he was despised and rejected of men, and that is an essential quality of the suffering of the cross. But this notion has ceased to be intelligible to a Christianity which can no longer see any difference between an ordinary human life and a life committed to Christ. The cross means sharing the suffering of Christ to the last and to the fullest. Only a man thus totally committed in discipleship can experience the meaning of the cross. The cross is there, right from the beginning, he has only got to pick it up; there is no need for him to go out and look for a cross for himself, no need for him deliberately to run after suffering. Jesus says that every Christian has his own cross waiting for him, a cross destined and appointed by God. Each must endure his allotted share of suffering and rejection. But each has a different share: some God deems worthy of the highest form of suffering, and gives them the grace of martyrdom, while others he does not allow to be tempted above what they are able to bear. But it is the one and the same cross in every case.

The cross is laid on every Christian. The first Christ-suffering which every man must experience is the call to abandon the attachments of this world. It is that dying of the old man which is the result of his encounter with Christ. As we embark upon discipleship we surrender ourselves to Christ in union with his death — we give over our lives to death. Thus it begins; the cross is not the terrible end to an otherwise god-fearing and happy life, but it meets us at the beginning of our communion with Christ. When Christ calls a man, he bids him come and die. It may be a death like that of the first disciples who had to leave home and work to follow him, or it may be a death like Luther's, who had to leave the monastery and go out into the world. But it is the same death every time — death in Jesus Christ, the death of the old man at his call. Jesus' summons to the rich young man was calling him to die, because only the man who is dead to his own will can follow Christ. In fact every command of Jesus is a call to die, with all our affections and lusts. But we do not want to die, and therefore Jesus Christ and his call are necessarily our death as well as our life. The call to discipleship, the baptism in the name of Jesus Christ means both death and life. The call of Christ, his baptism, sets the Christian in the middle of the daily arena against sin and the devil. Every day he encounters new temptation, and every day he must suffer anew for Jesus Christ's sake. The wounds and scars he receives in the fray are living tokens of this participation in the cross of his Lord. But there is another kind of suffering and shame which the Christian is not spared. While it is true that only the sufferings of Christ are a means of atonement, yet since he has suffered for and borne the sins of the whole world and shares with his disciples the fruits of his passion, the Christian also has to undergo temptation, he too has to bear the sins of others; he too must bear their shame and be driven like a scapegoat from the gate of the city. But he would certainly break down under this burden, but for the support of him who bore the sins of all. The passion of Christ strengthens him to overcome the sins of others by forgiving them. He becomes the bearer of other men's burdens — "Bear ye one another's burdens, and so fulfill the law of Christ" (Gal. 6:2). As Christ bears our burdens, so ought we to bear the burdens of our fellowmen. The law of Christ, which it is our duty to fulfill, is the bearing of the cross. My brother's burden which I must bear is not only his outward lot, his natural characteristics and gifts, but quite literally his sin. And the only way to bear that sin is by forgiving it in the power of the cross of Christ in which I now share. Thus the call to follow Christ always means a call to share the work of forgiving men their sins. Forgiveness is the Christlike suffering which it is the Christian's duty to bear.

But how is the disciple to know what kind of cross is meant for him? He will find out as soon as he begins to follow his Lord and to share his life.

Suffering, then, is the badge of true discipleship. The disciple is not above his master. Following Christ means *passio passiva,* suffering because we have to suffer. That is why Luther reckoned suffering among the marks of the true church, and one of the memoranda drawn up in preparation for the Augsburg Confession similarly defines the church as the community of those "who are persecuted and martyred for the gospel's sake." If we refuse to take up our cross and submit to suffering and rejection at the hands of men, we forfeit our fellowship with Christ and have ceased to follow him. But if we lose our lives in his service and carry our cross, we shall find our lives again in the fellowship of the cross with Christ. The opposite of discipleship is to be ashamed of Christ and his cross and all the offense which the cross brings in its train.

Discipleship means allegiance to the suffering Christ, and it is therefore not at all surprising that Christians should be called upon to suffer. In fact it is a joy and a token of his grace. The acts of the early Christian martyrs are full of evidence which shows how Christ transfigures for his own the hour of their mortal agony by granting them the unspeakable assurance of his presence. In the hour of the cruelest torture they bear for his sake, they are made partakers in the perfect joy and bliss of fellowship with him. To bear the cross proves to be the only way of triumphing over suffering. This is true for all who follow Christ, because it was true for him.

And he went forward a little, and fell on his face, and prayed, saying, O my Father, if it be possible, let this cup pass away from me; nevertheless, not as I will, but as thou wilt.... Again a second time he went away, and prayed, saying, O my Father, if this cannot pass away, except I drink it, thy will be done. (Matt. 26:39, 42)

Jesus prays to his Father that the cup may pass from him, and his Father hears his prayer; for the cup of suffering will indeed pass from him — *but only by his drinking it.* That is the assurance he receives as he kneels for the second time in the garden of Gethsemane that suffering will indeed pass as he accepts it. That is the only path to victory. The cross is his triumph over suffering.

Suffering means being cut off from God. Therefore those who live in communion with him cannot really suffer. This Old Testament doctrine was expressly reaffirmed by Jesus. That is why he takes upon himself the suffering of the whole world, and in doing so proves victorious over it. He bears the whole burden of man's separation from God, and in the very act of drinking the cup he causes it to pass over him. He sets out to overcome the suffering of the world, and so he must drink it to the dregs. Hence while it is still true that suffering means being cut off from God, yet within the fellowship of Christ's suffering, suffering is overcome by suffering, and becomes the way to communion with God.

Suffering has to be endured in order that it may pass away. Either the world must bear the whole burden and collapse beneath it, or it must fall on Christ to be overcome in him. He therefore suffers vicariously for the world. His is the only suffering which has redemptive efficacy. But the church knows that the world is still seeking for someone to bear its sufferings, and so, as it follows Christ, suffering becomes the church's lot too, and bearing it, it is borne up by Christ. As it follows him beneath the cross, the church stands before God as the representative of the world.

For God is a God who *bears*. The Son of God bore our flesh, he bore the cross, he bore our sins, thus making atonement for us. In the same way his followers are also called upon to bear, and that is precisely what it means to be a Christian. Just as Christ maintained his communion with the Father by his endurance, so his followers are to maintain their communion with Christ by their endurance. We can of course shake off the burden which is laid upon us, but only find that we have a still heavier burden to carry — a yoke of our own choosing, the yoke of our self. But Jesus invites all who travail and are heavy laden to throw off their own yoke and take his yoke upon them — and his yoke is easy, and his burden is light. The yoke and the burden of Christ are his cross. To go one's way under the sign of the cross is not misery and desperation, but peace and refreshment for the soul; it is the highest joy. Then we do not walk under our self-made laws and burdens, but under the yoke of him who knows us and who walks under the yoke with us. Under his yoke we are certain of his nearness and communion. It is he whom the disciple finds as he lifts up his cross.

> Discipleship is not limited to what you can comprehend — it must transcend all comprehension. Plunge into the deep waters beyond your own comprehension, and I will help you to comprehend even as I do. Bewilderment is the true comprehension. Not to know where you are going is the true knowledge. My comprehension transcends yours. Thus Abraham went forth from his father and not knowing whither he went. He trusted himself to my knowledge, and cared not for his own, and thus he took the right road and came to his journey's end. Behold, that is the way of the cross. You cannot find it yourself, so you must let me lead you as though you were a blind man. Wherefore it is not you, no man, no living creature, but I myself, who instruct you by my word and Spirit in the way you should go. Not the work which you choose, not the suffering you devise, but the road which is clean contrary to all that you choose or contrive or desire — that is the road you must take. To that I call you and in that you must be my disciple. If you do that, there is the acceptable time and there your master is come. (Luther)

4

Life Together

The background for Life Together *was Bonhoeffer's experi-*
ence in 1935–37 of community life at Finkenwalde, a seminary
established to train pastors for the Confessing Church. Bon-
hoeffer was determined that seminary training should not focus
only on academic study but also on prayer, reflection on Scrip-
ture, and spiritual formation. Finkenwalde was closed by the
Gestapo in 1937. Life Together, *from which this chapter on*
"Community" is drawn, was published in 1939.

"How very good and pleasant it is when kindred live together in
unity!" (Ps. 133:1). In what follows we will take a look at several
directions and principles that the Holy Scriptures give us for life
together under the Word.

The Christian cannot simply take for granted the privilege of
living among other Christians. Jesus Christ lived in the midst of
his enemies. In the end all his disciples abandoned him. On the
cross he was all alone, surrounded by criminals and the jeering
crowds. He had come for the express purpose of bringing peace
to the enemies of God. So Christians, too, belong not in the seclu-
sion of a cloistered life but in the midst of enemies. There they
find their mission, their work, "To rule is to be in the midst of
your enemies. And whoever will not suffer this does not want
to be part of the rule of Christ; such a person wants to be among
friends and sit among the roses and lilies, not with the bad people
but the religious people. O you blasphemers and betrayers of

Christ! If Christ had done what you are doing, who would ever have been saved?" (Luther).

"Though I scattered them among the nations, yet in far countries they shall remember me" (Zech. 10:9). According to God's will, the Christian church is a scattered people, scattered like seed "to all the kingdoms of the earth" (Deut. 28:25). That is the curse and its promise. God's people must live in distant lands among the unbelievers, but they will be the seed of the kingdom of God in all the world.

"I will...gather them in. For I have redeemed them,...and they shall...return" (Zech. 10:8–9). When will that happen? It has happened in Jesus Christ, who died "to gather into one the dispersed children of God" (John 11:52), and ultimately it will take place visibly at the end of time when the angels of God will gather God's elect from the four winds, from one end of heaven to the other (Matt. 24:31). Until then, God's people remain scattered, held together in Jesus Christ alone, having become one because they remember *him* in the distant lands, spread out among the unbelievers.

Thus in the period between the death of Christ and the day of Judgment, when Christians are allowed to live here in visible community with other Christians, we have merely a gracious anticipation of the end time. It is by God's grace that a congregation is permitted to gather visibly around God's word and sacrament in this world. Not all Christians partake of this grace. The imprisoned, the sick, the lonely who live in the diaspora, the proclaimers of the gospel in heathen lands stand alone. They know that visible community is grace. They pray with the psalmist: "I went with the throng, and led them in procession to the house of God, with glad shouts and songs of thanksgiving, a multitude keeping festival" (Ps. 42:5). But they remain alone in distant lands, a scattered seed according to God's will. Yet what is denied them as a visible experience they grasp more ardently in faith. Hence "in the Spirit on the Lord's Day" (Rev. 1:10) the exiled disciple of the Lord, John the author of the Apocalypse, celebrates the worship of heaven with its congregation in the loneliness of the Island of Patmos. He sees the seven lampstands that are the congregations, the seven stars that are the angels of the congregations, and in the midst and above it all, the Son of Man, Jesus Christ, in his great glory as the risen one. He strengthens and comforts John by his word. That is the heavenly community in which the exile participates on the day of his Lord's resurrection.

The physical presence of other Christians is a source of incomparable joy and strength to the believer. With great yearning the imprisoned apostle Paul calls his "beloved son in the faith": Timothy, to come to him in prison in the last days of his life. He wants to see him again and have him near. Paul has not forgotten the tears Timothy shed during their final parting (2 Tim. 1:4). Thinking of the congregation in Thessalonica, Paul prays "night and day...most earnestly that we may see you face to face" (1 Thess. 3:10). The aged John knows his joy in his own people will be complete only when he can come to them and speak to them face to face instead of using paper and ink (2 John 12). The believer need not feel any shame when yearning for the physical presence of other Christians, as if one were still living too much in the flesh. A human being is created as a body; the Son of God appeared on earth in the body for our sake and was raised in the body. In the sacrament the believer receives the Lord Christ in the body, and the resurrection of the dead will bring about the perfected community of God's spiritual-physical creatures. Therefore, the believer praises the Creator, the Reconciler, and the Redeemer, God the Father, Son, and Holy Spirit, for the bodily presence of the other Christians. The prisoner, the sick person, the Christian living in the diaspora recognizes in the nearness of a fellow Christian a physical sign of the gracious presence of the triune God. In their loneliness, both the visitor and the one visited recognize in each other the Christ who is present in the body. They receive and meet each other as one meets the Lord, in reverence, humility, and joy. They receive each other's blessings as the blessing of the Lord Jesus Christ. But if there is so much happiness and joy even in a single encounter of one Christian with another, what inexhaustible riches must invariably open up for those who by God's will are privileged to live in daily community life with other Christians! Of course, what is an inexpressible blessing from God for the lonely individual is easily disregarded and trampled under foot by those who receive the gift every day. It is easily forgotten that the community of Christians is a gift of grace from the kingdom of God, a gift that can be taken from us any day — that the time still separating us from the most profound loneliness may be brief indeed. Therefore, let those who until now have had the privilege of living a Christian life together with other Christians praise God's grace from the bottom of their hearts. Let them thank God on their knees and realize: it is grace, nothing but grace, that we are still permitted to live in the community of Christians today. . . .

Christian community means community through Jesus Christ and in Jesus Christ. There is no Christian community that is more than this, and none that is less than this. Whether it be a brief, single encounter or the daily community of many years, Christian community is solely this. We belong to one another only through and in Jesus Christ.

What does that mean? It means, *first,* that a Christian needs others for the sake of Jesus Christ. It means, *second,* that a Christian comes to others only through Jesus Christ. It means, *third,* that from eternity we have been chosen in Jesus Christ, accepted in time, and united for eternity.

First, Christians are persons who no longer seek their salvation, their deliverance, their justification in themselves, but in Jesus Christ alone. They know that God's Word in Jesus Christ pronounces them guilty, even when they feel nothing of their own guilt, and that God's Word in Jesus Christ pronounces them free and righteous, even when they feel nothing of their own righteousness. Christians no longer live by their own resources, by accusing themselves and justifying themselves, but by God's accusation and God's justification. They live entirely by God's Word pronounced on them, in faithful submission to God's judgment, whether it declares them guilty or righteous. The death and life of Christians are not situated in a self-contained isolation. Rather, Christians encounter both death and life only in the Word that comes to them from the outside, in God's Word to them. The Reformers expressed it by calling our righteousness an "alien righteousness," a righteousness that comes from outside of us (*extra nos*). They meant by this expression that Christians are dependent on the Word of God spoken to them. They are directed outward to the Word coming to them. Christians live entirely by the truth of God's Word in Jesus Christ. If they are asked "where is your salvation, your blessedness, your righteousness?" they can never point to themselves. Instead, they point to the Word of God in Jesus Christ that grants them salvation, blessedness, and righteousness. They watch for this Word wherever they can. Because they daily hunger and thirst for righteousness, they long for the redeeming Word again and again. It can only come from the outside. In themselves they are destitute and dead. Help must come from the outside; and it has come and comes daily and anew in the Word of Jesus Christ, bringing us redemption, righteousness, innocence, and blessedness. But God put this Word into the mouth of human beings so that it may be passed on to others. When people are deeply affected by the Word, they tell it to other people. God has willed that we should seek and find God's living Word in the testimony of other Christians, in the mouths of human beings. Therefore, Christians need other Christians who speak God's Word to them....

Second, a Christian comes to others only through Jesus Christ. Among human beings there is strife. "He is our peace" (Eph. 2:14), says Paul of Jesus Christ. In him, broken and divided humanity has become one. Without Christ there is discord between God and humanity and between one human being and another. Christ has become the mediator who has made peace with God and peace among human beings. Without Christ we would not know God; we could neither call on God nor come to God. Moreover, without Christ we would not know other Christians around us; nor could we approach them. The way to them is blocked by one's own ego. Christ opened up the way to God and to one another. Now Christians can live with each other in peace; they can love and serve one another; they can become one. But they can continue to do so only through Jesus Christ. Only in Jesus Christ are we one; only through him are we bound together. He remains the one and only mediator throughout eternity.

Third, when God's Son took on flesh, he truly and bodily, out of pure grace, took on our being, our nature, ourselves. This was the eternal decree of the triune God. Now we are in him. Wherever he is, he bears our flesh, he bears us. And, where he is, there we are too — in the incarnation, on the cross, and in his resurrection. We belong to him because we are in him. That is why the Scriptures call us the body of Christ. But if we have been elected and accepted with the whole church in Jesus Christ before we could know it or want it, then we also belong to Christ in eternity with one another. We who live here in community with Christ will one day be with Christ in eternal community. Those who look at other Christians should know that they will be eternally united with them in Jesus Christ. Christian community means community through and in Jesus Christ. Everything the Scriptures provide in the way of directions and rules for Christians' life together rests on this presupposition....

What persons are in themselves as Christians, in their inwardness and piety, cannot constitute the basis of our community, which is determined by what those persons are in terms of Christ. Our community consists solely in what Christ has done for both of us. That not only is true at the beginning, as if in the course of time something else were to be added to our community, but also remains so for all the future and into all eternity. I have community with others and will continue to have it only through Jesus Christ. The more genuine and the deeper our community becomes, the more everything else between us will recede, and the more clearly and purely will Jesus Christ and his work become the one and only thing that is alive between us. We have one another only through Christ, but through Christ we really do *have* one another. We have one another completely and for all eternity.

This dismisses at the outset every unhappy desire for something more. Those who want more than what Christ has established between us do not want Christian community. They are looking for some extraordinary experiences of community that were denied them elsewhere. Such people are bringing confused and tainted desires into the Christian community. Precisely at this point Christian community is most often threatened from the very outset by the greatest danger, the danger of internal poisoning, the danger of confusing Christian community with some wishful image of pious community, the danger of blending the devout heart's natural desire for community with the spiritual reality of Christian community. It is essential for Christian community that two things become clear right from the beginning. *First, Christian community is not an ideal, but a divine reality; second, Christian community is a spiritual [pneumatische] and not a psychic [psychische] reality.*

On innumerable occasions a whole Christian community has been shattered because it has lived on the basis of a wishful image. Certainly serious Christians who are put in a community for the first time will often bring with them a very definite image of what Christian communal life should be, and they will be anxious to realize it. But God's grace quickly frustrates all such dreams. A great disillusionment with others, with Christians in general, and, if we are fortunate, with ourselves, is bound to overwhelm us as surely as God desires to lead us to an understanding of genuine Christian community. By sheer grace God will not permit us to live in a dream world even for a few weeks and to abandon ourselves to those blissful experiences and exalted moods that sweep over us like a wave of rapture. For God is not a God of emotionalism, but the God of truth. Only that community which enters into the experience of this great disillusionment with all its unpleasant and evil appearances begins to be what it should be in God's sight, begins to grasp in faith the promise that is given to it. The sooner this moment of disillusionment comes over the individual and the community, the better for both. However, a community that cannot bear and cannot survive such disillusionment, clinging instead to its idealized image, when that should be done away with, loses at the same time the promise of a durable Christian community. Sooner or later it is bound to collapse. Every human idealized image that is brought into the Christian community is a hindrance to genuine community and must be broken up so that genuine community can survive. Those who love their dream of a Christian community more than the Christian community itself become destroyers of that Christian community even though their personal intentions may be ever so honest, earnest, and sacrificial.

God hates this wishful dreaming because it makes the dreamer proud and pretentious. Those who dream of this idealized community demand that it be fulfilled by God, by others, and by themselves. They enter the community of Christians with their demands, set up their own law, and judge one another and even God accordingly. They stand adamant, a living reproach to all others in the circle of the community. They act as if they have to create the Christian community, as if their visionary ideal binds the people together. Whatever does not go their way, they call a failure. When their idealized image is shattered, they set the community breaking into pieces. So they first become accusers of other Christians in the community, then accusers of God, and finally the desperate accusers of themselves. Because God already has laid the only foundation of our community, because God has united us in one body with other Christians in Jesus Christ long before we entered into common life with them, we enter into that life together with other Christians, not as those who make demands, but as those who thankfully receive. We thank God for what God has done for us. We thank God for giving us other Christians who live by God's call, forgiveness, and promise. We do not complain about what God does not give us; rather we are thankful for what God does give us daily. And is not what has been given us enough: other believers who will go on living with us through sin and need under the blessing of God's grace? Is the gift of God any less immeasurably great than this on any given day, even on the most difficult and distressing days of a Christian community? Even when sin and misunderstanding burden the common life, is not the one who sins still a person with whom I too stand under the word of Christ? Will not another Christian's sin be an occasion for me ever anew to give thanks that both of us may live in the forgiving love of God in Jesus Christ? Therefore, will not the very moment of great disillusionment with my brother or sister be incomparably wholesome for me because it so thoroughly teaches me that both of us can never live by our own words and deeds, but only by that one Word and deed that really binds us together, the forgiveness of sins in Jesus Christ? The bright day of Christian community dawns wherever the early morning mists of dreamy visions are lifting....

Like the Christian's sanctification, Christian community is a gift of God to which we have no claim. Only God knows the real condition of either our community or our sanctification. What may appear weak and insignificant to us may be great and glorious to God. Just as Christians should not be constantly feeling the pulse of their spiritual life, so too the Christian community has not been given to us by God for us to be continually taking its temperature. The more thankfully we daily receive what is given to us, the more assuredly and consistently will community increase and grow from day to day as God pleases.

Christian community is not an ideal we have to realize, but rather a reality created by God in Christ in which we may participate. The more clearly we learn to recognize that the ground and strength and promise of all our community is in Jesus Christ alone, the more calmly we will learn to think about our community and pray and hope for it....

Two factors, which are really one and the same thing, reveal the difference between spiritual and self-centered love. Emotional, self-centered love cannot tolerate the dissolution of a community that has become false, even for the sake of genuine community. And such self-centered love cannot love an enemy, that is to say, one who seriously and stubbornly resists it. Both spring from the same source: emotional love is by its very nature desire, desire for self-centered community. As long as it can possibly satisfy this desire, it will not give it up, even for the sake of truth, even for the sake of genuine love for others. But emotional, self-centered love is at an end when it can no longer expect its desire to be fulfilled, namely, in the face of an enemy. There it turns into hatred, contempt, and slander.

Spiritual love, however, begins right at this point. This is why emotional, self-centered love turns into personal hatred when it encounters genuine spiritual love that does not desire but serves. Self-centered love makes itself an end in itself. It turns itself into an achievement, an idol it worships, to which it must subject everything. It cares for, cultivates, and loves itself and nothing else in the world. Spiritual love, however, comes from Jesus Christ; it serves him alone. It knows that it has no direct access to other persons. Christ stands between me and others. I do not know in advance what love of others means on the basis of the general idea of love that grows out of my emotional desires. All this may instead be hatred and the worst kind of selfishness in the eyes of Christ. Only Christ in his Word tells me what love is. Contrary to all my own opinions and convictions, Jesus Christ will tell me what love for my brothers and sisters really looks like. Therefore, spiritual love is bound to the word of Jesus Christ alone. Where Christ tells me to maintain community for the sake of love, I desire to maintain it. Where the truth of Christ orders me to dissolve a community for the sake of love, I will dissolve it, despite all the protests of my self-centered love. Because spiritual love does not desire but rather serves, it loves an enemy as a brother or sister. It originates neither in the brother or sister nor in the enemy, but in Christ and his word. Self-centered, emotional love can never comprehend spiritual love, for spiritual love is from above. It is something completely strange, new, and incomprehensible to all earthly love.

Because Christ stands between me and an other, I must not long for unmediated community with that person. As only Christ was able to speak to me in such a way that I was helped, so others too can only be helped by Christ alone. However, this means that I must release others from all my attempts to control, coerce, and dominate them with my love. In their freedom from me, other persons want to be loved for who they are, as those for whom Christ became a human being, died, and rose again, as those for whom Christ won the forgiveness of sins and prepared eternal life. Because Christ has long since acted decisively for other Christians, before I could begin to act, I must allow them the freedom to be Christ's. They should encounter me only as the persons that they already are for Christ. This is the meaning of the claim that we can encounter others only through the mediation of Christ. Self-centered love constructs its own image of other persons, about what they are and what they should become. It takes the life of the other person into its own hands. Spiritual love recognizes the true image of the other person as seen from the perspective of Jesus Christ. It is the image Jesus Christ has formed and wants to form in all people....

The existence of any Christian communal life essentially depends on whether or not it succeeds at the right time in promoting the ability to distinguish between a human ideal and God's reality, between spiritual and emotional community. The life and death of a Christian community is decided by its ability to reach sober clarity on these points as soon as possible. In other words, a life together under the Word will stay healthy only when it does not form itself into a movement, an order, a society, a *collegium pietatis,* but instead understands itself as being part of the one, holy, universal, Christian church, sharing through its deeds and suffering in the hardships and struggles and promise of the whole church. Every principle of selection, and every division connected with it that is not necessitated quite objectively by common work, local conditions, or family connections is of the greatest danger to a Christian community. Self-centeredness always insinuates itself in any process of intellectual or spiritual selectivity, destroying the spiritual power of the community and robbing the community of its effectiveness for the church, thus driving it into sectarianism. The exclusion of the weak and insignificant, the seemingly useless people, from everyday Christian life in community may actually mean the exclusion of Christ; for in the poor sister or brother, Christ is knocking at the door. We must, therefore, be very careful on this point....

There is probably no Christian to whom God has not given the uplifting and blissful *experience* of genuine Christian community at least once in her or his life. But in this world such experiences remain nothing but a gracious extra beyond the daily bread of Christian community life. We have no claim to such experiences, and we do not live with other Christians for the sake of gaining such experiences. It is not the experience of Christian community, but firm and certain faith within Christian community that holds us together. We hold fast in faith to God's greatest gift, that God has acted for us all and wants to act for us all. This makes us joyful and happy, but it also makes us ready to forgo all such experiences if at times God does not grant them. We are bound together by faith, not by experience.

"How very good and pleasant it is when kindred live together in unity." This is the Scripture's praise of life together under the Word. But now we can correctly interpret the words "in unity" and say "when kindred live together through Christ." For Jesus Christ alone is our unity. "He is our peace." We have access to one another, joy in one another, community with one another through Christ alone.

5

Pastor of the Confessing Church

The selections in this chapter reflect Bonhoeffer's role as pastor of the Confessing Church. With the closure of the seminary at Finkenwalde in 1937 the Confessing Church had effectively ceased to exist as an institution. In general Bonhoeffer felt that the Confessing Church had capitulated all too quickly and failed to present effective resistance to the encroaching atmosphere of oppression. Still he attempted through his preaching and circular letters to encourage the scattered brethren to maintain courage, faith, and hope. These texts are reprinted from A Testament to Freedom: The Essential Writings of Dietrich Bonhoeffer.

TO THE YOUNG BROTHERS
OF THE CHURCH IN POMERANIA

The end of January 1938

Dear Brothers:

During the past few weeks, letters and personal comments have reached me which make it clear that our church, and in Pomerania particularly our group of young theologians, has come to a time of sore trial. It is no longer a question of the troubles of one individual, for a great many people are being threatened by one and the same temptation, so I hope that you won't mind if I try to give a common answer to you all. Of course, the letter is still meant for each of you personally. I shall try to take up all the points that you have severally made, in the course of it.

We have to cover a great deal of ground. We shall all agree that when we embraced the cause of the Confessing Church we took the step with a supreme faith which was, for that very reason, a boldness beyond human understanding. We were glad, certain of victory, ready for sacrifice. Our whole life, both our personal life and our ministry, had taken a new turn. Of course I don't pretend that there weren't all sorts of purely human overtones to our feelings — who knows even his own heart? — but there was one thing that made us so joyful and ready to fight and even ready to suffer. Once again we knew that a life with Jesus Christ and his church is worth staking everything on. We believed that in the Confessing Church we had not only found, but through God's great goodness had also actually experienced, the church of Jesus Christ. For individuals, for pastors, and for communities, a new life began in the joy of God's Word. As long as God's Word was with us, we no longer wanted to worry and fret about the future. With this Word we were ready to fight, to suffer, to undergo poverty, sin, and death, so as finally to reach God's kingdom. Young people and the fathers of large families stood here side by side. What was it that united us then and gave us such great joy? It was the one, age-old recognition which God himself had granted us again, that Jesus Christ wants to build his church among us, a church which lives only by the preaching of the pure, untainted gospel and the grace of his Sacraments, a church which obeys him alone in everything that it does. Christ himself will stand by a church like this; he will protect and guide it. Only a church like this can be free from all fear. This, and nothing else, was acknowledged by the synods of the Confessing Church at Barmen and at Dahlem. Was it an illusion? Did the synods speak under the pressure of external circumstances, which seemed favorable to a "realization" of this faith? No, it was supreme faith, it was the biblical truth itself and was clearly acknowledged then before the whole world. The witness of Christ conquered our hearts, made us glad, and summoned us to act obediently. Dear brothers, surely we are at least agreed on this much, that this was the case?

Or do we now want to abuse the grace of God which he has so richly given to us?

That, then, was the beginning of the fight for the true church of Christ. Or do you perhaps think that the devil took all that trouble to annihilate a band of rabid idealists? No, Christ was in the ship, and so the storm was stilled. The battle demanded sacrifice from the beginning. Perhaps everyone did not always realize how much both individuals and communities would have to give up so that the members of the Councils of Brethren would be able to fulfill their duty to the church. But the sacrifices were joyfully made for the cause of Jesus Christ. Who could hold back as long as Jesus still called, "Be the church. Be the church that serves none but me?" Who could take his leave as long as no one released him from his responsibility to preach the pure gospel and to build up the communities in accordance with Scripture and the confessions of our church?

If we are still in agreement here, too, then let us ask in all openness what has happened between those beginnings and our present situation. Perhaps we might put it another way. What is the difference between the church in those provinces where men still live and work and fight as they did at the beginning, and the church in our province? Why has there been incessant lamentation in Pomerania for several months that our church is paralyzed, that it is under a curse, that an inner narrowness and stubbornness is preventing us from doing fruitful work? How has it happened that brethren who were convinced members of the Confessing Church are now saying that all their joy has gone? That they see no good reason why they could not do their work as well under the consistory of the national church as under the Council of Brethren? And can we deny that the witness of our church in Pomerania has recently been growing weaker and weaker? Can we deny that the word of the Confessing Church has largely lost its power to awaken belief and thus call for a decision? Who can deny that the real theological decisions of the church are continually being obscured by considerations of expediency? And has not all this had its effect on our own preaching, too? We ask why all this happens. I don't think that the answer is as hard as people make out. The so-called paralysis in the Confessing Church, the lack of joy, the weak witness, comes from our own disobedience. We should not be thinking about other people now, but about ourselves and our work. What has become of the first clear decisions of the Confessing Church in our communities? ...

Let me try to put it in a different way: the church struggle can be law or gospel. At the moment it has largely become law as far as we are concerned. We rebel against it. It has become a threatening, angry law which strikes us down. No man can support and direct the church struggle as law without succumbing to it and failing completely. As law, the church struggle is without joy, without certainty, without authority, and without promise. How is that? It is just the same here as in our personal lives. If through our disobedience we evade the gracious Word of God, it becomes a harsh law for us. What is a gentle and easy yoke when done in obedience becomes an insupportable burden when done in disobedience. The more we have hardened ourselves in disobedience against the gracious Word, the harder it is to change, the more obstinately we rebel against God's claim. But just as in our personal life there is only one way, the way of repentance, of patience under God's Word, in which God restores to us our lost communion, so too it is in the church struggle. Without penitence, i.e., unless the church struggle itself becomes our penitence, we shall never receive back the gift we have lost, the church struggle as gospel. Even if the obedience of penitence is harder now than it was then, because we are hardened in our guilt — it is the only way by which God will help us back to the right road....

In the past week we have shared a meditation text from Haggai 1; it runs: "This people say, 'The time has not yet come to rebuild the house of the Lord.' Then the Word of the Lord came by Haggai the prophet, 'Is it a time for you yourselves to dwell in your paneled houses, while this house lies in ruins?'" (Hag. 1:2–4). It is none of my business, as they say, to "straighten you out," to convince you. But everything does of course depend on our reawakening in you, with God's Word, the courage, the joy, the faith, in Jesus Christ who is and will remain with the Confessing Church, whether you go along with it or not. You ought to know that the faith which threatens to become extinguished among you still lives as it did in the beginning in many communities and many pastorates, that solitary brethren, in Pomerania and outside, in lonely outposts, bear witness to this faith with the greatest joy. The church of Jesus Christ, which lives only from his Word and which means to be obedient to him alone in all things, still lives and will live, and calls you back from temptation and trial. It calls you to penitence and warns you for the unfaithfulness which must ultimately end in despair. It prays for you, that your faith may not fail....

You no longer hope for the success of the Confessing Church. You cannot see any way out. Indeed, who among us *can* see a way out? Only God can do that, and he will show it to those who humbly wait for it. Perhaps we once hoped that the Confessing Church would gain public recognition in Germany. But was this hope ever promised? Certainly not. Now we have learned to believe in a church which follows its Lord beneath the cross. That is more like the promise. Finally, you say that you would be ready for all kinds of sacrifice both personally and in your ministry, if only you knew why they were necessary. Why, dear brethren? For no reason that men can see, not for the sake of a flourishing church or of a convincing church government, but simply because the way of the Confessing Church must also be followed through desolate stretches of desert and wilderness and because you do not want to stay in the wilderness. So for the sake of the poor church, which will of course go on under the guidance of its Lord even without you, for the sake of your faith, for your certainty, you should remain with the Confessing Church....

THE SECRET OF SUFFERING
Finkenwalde, March 1938

Therefore, being justified by faith, we have peace with God through our Lord Jesus Christ. Through him we have attained access to this grace in which we stand, and we rejoice in our hope of sharing the glory of God. More than that, we rejoice in our sufferings, knowing that suffering produces perseverance, and perseverance produces character, and character produces hope, and hope does not disappoint us, because God's love has been poured into our hearts through the Holy Spirit which has been given to us. (Rom. 5:1–5)

"We have peace with God." So, our struggle with God is over now. Our obstinate hearts have yielded to God's will, and our own desires have subsided. It is God's victory, and our flesh and blood, which hate God, have been broken and must keep quiet. "Therefore, being justified by faith, we have peace with God." God was right in the end. In the song we have just sung, we say, "You are just, come what may." God is just, whether or not we understand his ways; God is just, whether he corrects and chastises us or pardons us. God is just; we are the transgressors. We don't see it, but our faith must acknowledge: God alone is just. Whoever acknowledges by faith that God is right in judging him has come into the right position before God; he is well prepared to be able to stand in the presence of God; he has been justified by his faith in God's justice, he has found peace with God.

"We have peace with God through our Lord Jesus Christ." Now God's fight against us is also at an end. God hated that will that refused to submit itself to him. He called, admonished, entreated, and threatened, countless times, until his wrath over us knew no more patience. In that moment, he prepared to let loose a blow against us; he let us have it and hit the mark. He struck the only innocent person on earth. It was his beloved Son, our Lord Jesus Christ. Jesus Christ died for us on the cross, struck by God's wrath. God himself sent him for that purpose. When his Son submitted to his will and authority unto death, then God's wrath was satisfied. Wonderful mystery — God had made peace with us through Jesus Christ.

"We have peace with God." Beneath the cross is peace. Here is surrender to God's will; here is the end of our own will; here is rest and tranquility in God; here is peace of conscience in the forgivcncss of all our sins. Here beneath the cross is the "access into the grace wherein we stand," the daily acccss to peace with God. Here is the way that is provided in the world to find peace with God. In Jesus Christ, God's wrath is satisfied, while we are overcome in God's will. That is why, for his congregation, Jesus' cross is an eternal foundation of joy and hope in the coming glory of God. "We rejoice in hope of the glory of God." Here at the cross, God's justice and victory have dawned on earth. Here he will become known to all thc world one day. The peace that we receive here will become an eternal, glorious peace in the kingdom of God.

But while we would like most of all to stop here, filled with the greatest joy that human beings can be granted on this earth; filled, that is, filled with the knowledge of God in Jesus Christ, with the peace of God in the cross, Scripture will not yet let us go. "And not only so," it says now. It hasn't all been said yet, after all. But what more could remain to be said after the cross of Jesus Christ and the peace of God in Jesus Christ have been spoken of? Yes, dear friends, there is still a word to be said; namely, a word about you, a word about your life beneath the cross, a word about how God is going to test your life in the peace of God, so that the peace of God will not be merely a word, but a reality. There is still a word to be said; that you will live a while longer on this earth, and about how you will preserve the peace of God.

Therefore our text tells us, "And not only so, but we glory in tribulations also." The test of whether we have truly found the peace of God will be in how we face the sufferings which befall us. There are many Christians who bend their knees before the cross of Jesus Christ well enough, but who do nothing but rcsist and struggle against every affliction in their own lives. They believe that they love Christ's cross, but they hate the cross in their own lives. In reality, therefore, they hate the cross of Jesus Christ as well; in reality, they are despisers of the cross, who for their part, seek to flee the cross by whatever means they can. Whoever knows that he regards suffering and trouble in his own life as something wholly hostile, wholly evil, can know by this that he has not yet found peace with God at all. Actually, he has only sought peace with the world, thinking perhaps that he could cope with himself and all his questions with the cross of Jesus Christ; in other words, that he could find an inner peace of mind. Thus, he needed the cross, but did not love it. He sought peace only for his own sake. When sufferings come, however, this peace quickly disappears. It was no peace with God because he hated the sufferings God sends.

Thus, whoever feels only hate for the sufferings, sacrifice, want, slander, and captivity in his life, however eloquently he may otherwise speak about the cross, he hates Jesus' cross and has no peace with God. But whoever loves the cross of Jesus Christ, whoever has found peace in him, he begins to love even the sufferings in his life, and in the end, he will be able to say with Scripture, "We also rejoice in our sufferings."

Our church has suffered many a tribulation in recent years. As of this hour: destruction of its order, the penetration of a false preaching, much hostility, evil words, and slander, imprisonment, and every kind of affliction, and no one knows what sufferings still await the church. But through all that, we have also realized that God himself intended thereby, and still intends, to put us to the test, that in all that has happened, only one question has been important, namely, do we have peace with God, or have we lived up to now in an entirely worldly peace?

How much grumbling and resisting, how much opposition to, and hatred of, our sufferings, has that revealed within us, and how much betrayal of our own principles, how much standing aside, how much fear, when Jesus' cross so much as begins to cast a tiny shadow on our own lives? How often have we thought that we could well preserve our peace with God, and yet avoid the suffering, the sacrifice, the hatred, the threats to our existence! Yes, worst of all, haven't we had to hear over and over again from Christian brothers and sisters that they despise their suffering? — and for the sole reason that their own consciences give them no peace of mind.

But God will take no one into his kingdom whose faith he has not proved as genuine in tribulation. "We *must* through much tribulation enter into the kingdom of God." Therefore, we should learn to grow fond of our sufferings before it is too late; yes, we should learn to rejoice and boast in them.

How is that to happen? "We know that suffering produces perseverance; perseverance, character; and character, hope. And hope does not disappoint us." In this way, we learn for the first time from God's word how we should look at and understand sufferings. The sufferings, which appear so hard and objectionable to us in our lives, are in reality full of the greatest treasures a Christian can find. They are like the shell in which a pearl rests. They are like a deep shaft, in which, the deeper one climbs down inside, the more things one finds: first ore, then silver, and finally gold. Suffering produces first perseverance, then character, then hope. Whoever avoids suffering rejects with it God's greatest gift for those who belong to him.

"Suffering produces perseverance." Perseverance, translated literally, means: remaining underneath, not throwing off the load, but bearing it. We know much too little in the church today about the peculiar blessing of bearing. Bearing, not shaking off; bearing, but not collapsing either; bearing as Christ bore the cross, remaining underneath, and there beneath it — to find Christ. If God imposes a load; then the one who perseveres bows his head and believes that it is good for him to be humbled — remain *underneath!* But *remaining* underneath. For remaining steadfast, remaining strong is meant here too; not weak acquiescence or surrender, no masochism, but growing stronger under the load, as under God's grace, imperturbably preserving the peace of God. God's peace is found with those who persevere.

"Perseverance produces character." A Christian life proves itself not in words, but character. No one is a Christian without character, Paul is talking here not about the experience of life, but about the experience of God. Nor is he talking about kinds of spiritual experiences, but rather about those experiences which arise in the trial of our faith and our peace with God, about the experience of Jesus' cross. Only those who persevere are experienced and produce character. Those who do not persevere experience nothing that will build character. To whomever

God wants to grant such experience — to an individual or to a church — to them he sends much temptation, restlessness, and anxiety; they must cry out daily and hourly for the peace of God. The experience that is talked of here leads us into the depths of hell, to the jaws of death, and into the night of unbelief. But through all of that, God does not want to take his peace from us. Throughout, we experience God's power and victory, and the ultimate peace at Christ's cross more with each passing day.

Therefore, character produces hope. For every temptation overcome is already the prelude to the last conquest; every wave surmounted brings us closer to the longed-for land. This is why hope grows with character; and in the experience of suffering, the reflection of eternal glory can be sensed already.

"And hope does not disappoint us." Where there is still hope, there is no defeat; there may be every kind of weakness, much clamor and complaining, much anxious shouting; nevertheless, because hope is present, the victory has already been won. This is the secret of suffering in the church and in the Christian life; precisely that gate on which it is written: "Abandon all hope," that gate of sorrow, of loss, and of death is to become for us the gate of great hope in God, the gate of splendor and glory. "And hope does not disappoint us." Do we still have this great hope in God himself in our church and for our church? Then everything is won. Do we no longer have it? Then everything is lost. "Suffering produces perseverance; perseverance, character; and character, hope; and hope does not disappoint us" — but all that is only for him who has found and preserves the peace of God in Jesus Christ, and about whom it is written: because God has poured out his love into our hearts by the Holy Spirit, whom he has given us. He who is loved by God, and who therefore loves God alone and above all things, only he is allowed to speak in this way. No, the series of steps from perseverance to hope is no self-evident truth gained by worldly experience. Luther said that it might very well be put in an entirely different manner; namely: suffering produces a lack of perseverance; a lack of perseverance, impenitence; and impenitence despair; and despair utterly disappoints us. Indeed, so it must be, when the peace of God is lost to us, when we prefer an earthly peace with the world to peace with God, when we love the certainties of our life more than we love God. Then suffering must prove to be our ruin.

But the love of God is poured out into our hearts. To whomever God grants, through the Holy Spirit, that the incomprehensible take place within him; that is, that he begins to love God for God's sake, not for the sake of worldly goods and gifts, not even for the sake of peace, but really for God's sake and his sake alone; whoever has encountered the love of God in the cross of Jesus Christ, so that he begins to love God for Jesus Christ's sake, whoever is led by the Holy Spirit to desire nothing more than to share in God's love for eternity, but other than that to desire nothing, nothing at all—such a person speaks out of this love of God's, and with him, the whole congregation of Jesus Christ: We have peace with God. We rejoice in our sufferings. The love of God is poured out into our hearts. Amen.

CHRISTUS VICTOR
Communion Address on Memorial Day
at the secret seminary, Wendisch-Tychow–Sigurdshof, November 26, 1939

Death is swallowed up in victory. O death where is thy sting? O grave, where is thy victory? (1 Cor. 15:34–55)

When death and life did battle, that was a singular strife. But death was overcome, and the victory won by life.

You are invited to a victory celebration, to the celebration of the greatest victory that has been won in the world, to the celebration of Jesus' victory over death. Bread and wine, body and blood of our Lord Jesus Christ, are the signs of victory; for in them, Jesus is present and alive today, the same man who was crucified on the cross and laid in the grave almost two thousand

years ago. Jesus arose from the dead; he forced open the tomb-
stone; Jesus remained the victor. You, however, are to receive the
signs of his victory today. And when you receive the blessed bread
and cup in just a short while, then you are to know at the same
time, as assuredly as I eat this bread and drink this wine, Jesus
Christ has remained victor over death, he is the living Lord who
meets us.

In our lives we don't speak readily of victory. It is too big a
word for us. We have suffered too many defeats in our lives;
victory has been thwarted again and again by too many weak
hours, too many gross sins. But isn't it true that the spirit within
us yearns for this word, for the final victory over the sin and anxious fear of death in our lives? And now God's Word also says
nothing to us about our victory; it doesn't promise us that *we*
will be victorious over sin and death from now on; rather, it says
with all its might that someone has won this victory, and that this
person, if we have him as Lord, will also win the victory over us.
It is not we who are victorious, but Jesus.

We proclaim that today and believe it despite all that we see
around us, despite the graves of our loved ones, despite the mori-
bund nature outside, despite the death that the war brings upon
us again. We see the supremacy of death; yet we proclaim and
believe the victory of Jesus Christ over death. Death is swallowed
up in victory. Jesus is the victor, the resurrection of the dead, and
the everlasting life.

That which Holy Scripture sings here is like an exultant, mock-
ing song about death and sin: O death, where is thy sting?
O grave, where is thy victory? We see death and sin puff themselves up and strike fear into the human heart as if they were still
lords of the world. But that is mere show. They lost their power
long ago. Jesus took it from them. Besides, no one who is with
Jesus need fear these sinister lords any longer. The sting of death,
which death uses to hurt us — that is sin — has no more power.
Hell can do no more against us, who are with Jesus. They are
powerless; they still rage, like a mean dog on a chain, but they
can do nothing against us, for Jesus holds them fast. He remains
the victor.

But if that is the case, we ask ourselves, then why does it seem so entirely different in our lives; why do we see so little of this victory? Why do sin and death rule over us so terribly? Indeed, this question is the very question God addresses to you: All that I have done for you, and you live as if nothing had happened! You submit to sin and the fear of death as if they could still enslave you! Why is there so little victory in your lives? Because you won't believe that Jesus is victor over death and sin, victor over your life. It is your unbelief that leads to your defeats. But now Jesus' victory is proclaimed to you once again today, at the Holy Communion; it is victory over sin and death for you, too, whoever you may be. Take hold of it in belief; today Jesus will once again forgive you all your serious and multiple sins, he will make you wholly pure and innocent, and from now on, you won't have to sin any more; sin won't have to rule over you anymore. Jesus will rule over you, and he is stronger than every temptation. In the hour of your temptation, and in your fear of death, Jesus will conquer you, and you will acknowledge: Jesus has become victor over my sin, over my death. As often as you give up this belief you will flounder and be defeated, sin and die; as often as you lay hold of this belief Jesus will have the victory.

On Memorial Day, we are asked at the graves of our loved ones: How do you intend to die one day? Do we believe in the power of death and sin, or do we believe in the power of Jesus Christ? Of the two there can be only one. In the last century, there was a man of God who had preached often in the course of his life about the victory of Jesus Christ, and who had done wonderful things. As he lay on his deathbed, as he lay in great torment and agony, his son bent down to his ear and cried out to the dying man: Father, victory is won. When dark hours come, and when the darkest hour comes upon us, then let us hear the voice of Jesus Christ, which cries in our ears: victory is won. Death is swallowed up in victory. Be comforted. And God grant that we may be able to say then: I believe in the forgiveness of sins, the resurrection of the body, and the life everlasting. In this belief, let us live and die. To that end, we take the Holy Communion. Amen.

ADVENT LETTER TO THE PASTORS
OF THE CONFESSING CHURCH

November 29, 1942

Dear Brothers:

At the head of a letter which is intended to summon you to joy at a serious hour must stand the names of the brothers who have been killed since last I wrote to you....

"With everlasting joy upon their heads..." (Isa. 35:10). We do not grudge it them; indeed, should we say that sometimes we envy them in the stillness? Since ancient times, *acidia* — sorrowfulness of the heart, "resignation" — has been one of the deadly sins. "Serve the Lord with gladness" (Ps. 100:2) summons us to the Scriptures. This is what our life has been given to us for, what it has been preserved for up till now. Joy belongs, not only to those who have been called home, but also to the living, and no one shall take it from us. We are one with them in this joy, but never in sorrow. How shall we be able to help those who have become joyless and fearful unless we ourselves are supported by courage and joy? I don't mean by this something fabricated, compelled, but something given, free. Joy dwells with God; it descends from him and seizes spirit, soul, and body, and where this joy has grasped a man it grows greater, carries him away, opens closed doors. There is a joy which knows nothing of sorrow, need, and anxiety of the heart; it has no duration, and it can only drug one for the moment. The joy of God has been through the poverty of the crib and the distress of the cross; therefore it is insuperable, irrefutable. It does not deny the distress where it is, but finds God in the midst of it, indeed precisely there; it does not contest the most grievous sin, but finds forgiveness in just this way; it looks death in the face, yet finds life in death itself. We are concerned with this joy which has overcome. It alone is worth believing; it alone helps and heals. The joy of our friends who have been called home is also the joy of those who have overcome — the risen one bears the marks of the cross upon his body; we are still engaged in conflict daily, they have overcome for all time. God alone knows how near to us or far from us stands the last overcoming, in which our own death can become joy. "With peace and joy I go hence...."

Some of us suffer a great deal from having our senses dulled in the face of all the sorrows which these war years have brought with them. Someone said to me recently: "I pray every day for my senses not to become dulled." That is certainly a good prayer. And yet we must be careful not to confuse ourselves with Christ. Christ endured all suffering and all human guilt to the full, indeed he was Christ in that he suffered everything alone. But Christ could suffer alongside people because at the same time he was able to redeem them from suffering. He had his power to suffer with people from his love and his power to redeem people. We are not called to burden ourselves with the sorrows of the whole world; in the end, we cannot suffer with people in our own strength because we are unable to redeem. A suppressed desire to suffer with someone in one's own strength must become resignation. We are simply called to look with utter joy on the one who really suffered with people and became their redeemer. We may joyfully believe that there was, there is, a man to whom no human sorrow and no human sin is strange and who in the profoundest love achieved our redemption. Only in such joy toward Christ, the Redeemer, are we saved from having our senses dulled by the pressure of human sorrow, or from becoming resigned under the experience of suffering. We believe in Christ only as much as...in Christ...[Letter incomplete].

6

Ethics

⚜

Bonhoeffer labored for several years over his Ethics, *a major work that remained in fragments at the time of his arrest. It was later edited by his friend Eberhard Bethge and published posthumously in 1949.*

LOVE

"And though I have the gift of prophecy, and understand all mysteries, and all knowledge; and though I have all faith, so that I could remove mountains, and have not love, I am nothing. And though I bestow all my goods to feed the poor, and though I give my body to be burned, and have not love, it profiteth me nothing" (1 Cor. 13:2 and 3). This is the decisive word which marks the distinction between man in disunion and man in the origin. The word is love. There is a recognition of Christ, a powerful faith in Christ, and indeed a conviction and a devotion of love even unto death — all without love. That is the point. Without this "love" everything falls apart and everything is inacceptable, but in this love everything is united and everything is pleasing to God. What is this love?

Everything that we have so far seen to be true excludes all those definitions which endeavor to represent the essence of love as a human attitude, as conviction, devotion, sacrifice, the will to fellowship, feeling, brotherhood, service, or action. All these, without exception, can, as we have just heard, arise without "love." Everything that we are accustomed to call love, that which lives in the depths of the soul and in the visible deed, and even the brotherly service of one's neighbor which proceeds from a pious heart, all this can be without "love," not because there is always a "residue" of selfishness in all human conduct, entirely overshadowing love, but because love as a whole is something entirely different from what the word designates here. Nor is love the direct relationship between persons, the acceptance of the personal and the individual in contrast to the law of the objective and impersonal institution. Quite apart from this thoroughly unbiblical and abstract wrenching apart of the "personal" and the "objective" or "real," love here becomes an attitude of man, and only a partial one at that. "Love" now becomes the superior ethos of the personal, which perfects and completes the inferior ethos of the purely real and institutional. It is, for example, in accordance with this view that one regards love and truth as mutually conflicting and gives priority to love as the personal principle over truth as the impersonal principle, thereby coming into direct contradiction with St. Paul's saying that love "rejoiceth in the truth" (1 Cor. 13:6). For indeed love knows nothing of the very conflict in terms of which one seeks to define it. On the contrary, it is of the essence of love that it should lie beyond all disunion. A love which violates or even merely neutralizes truth is called by Luther, with his clear biblical vision, an "accursed love," even though it may present itself in the most pious dress. A love which embraces only the sphere of personal human relations and which capitulates before the objective and real can never be the love of the New Testament.

If, then, there is no conceivable human attitude or conduct which, as such, can unequivocally be designated by the name of "love," if love lies beyond all the disunion in which man lives, and if at the same time anything that men can understand and practice as love is conceivable only as human conduct within this actual disunion, then it is an enigma and an open question what else the Bible can mean by "love." The Bible does not fail to give us the answer. We know this answer well enough, but we continually misinterpret it. It is this: "God is love" (1 John 4:16).

First of all, for the sake of clarity, this sentence is to be read with the emphasis on the word "God," whereas we have fallen into the habit of emphasizing the word "love." *God* is love; that is to say not a human attitude, a conviction or a deed, but God Himself is love. Only he who knows God knows what love is; it is not the other way round; it is not that we first of all by nature know what love is and therefore know also what God is. No one knows God unless God reveals Himself to him. And so no one knows what love is except in the self-revelation of God. Love, then, is the revelation of God. And the revelation of God is Jesus Christ. "In this was manifested the love of God toward us, because God sent his only begotten Son into the world, that we might live through him" (1 John 4:9). God's revelation in Jesus Christ, God's revelation of His love, precedes all our love toward Him. Love has its origin not in us but in God. Love is not an attitude of men but an attitude of God. "Herein is love, not that we loved God, but that he loved us and sent his Son to be the propitiation for our sins" (1 John 4:10). Only in Jesus Christ do we know what love is, namely, in His deed for us. "Hereby perceive we the love of God, because he laid down his life for us" (1 John 3:16). And even here there is given no general definition of love, in the sense, for example, of its being the laying down of one's life for the lives of others. What is here called love is not this general principle but the utterly unique event of the laying down of the life of Jesus Christ for us. Love is inseparably bound up with the name of Jesus Christ as the revelation of God. The New Testament answers the question "What is love?" quite unambiguously by pointing solely and entirely to Jesus Christ. He is the only definition of love. But again it would be a complete misunderstanding if we were to derive a general definition of love from our view of Jesus Christ and of His deed and His suffering. Love is not what He *does* and what He *suffers,* but it is what *He* does and what *He* suffers. Love is always He Himself. Love is always God Himself. Love is always the revelation of God in Jesus Christ.

When all our ideas and principles relating to love are concentrated in the strictest possible manner upon the name of Jesus

Christ, this must, above all, not be allowed to reduce this name to a mere abstract concept. This name must always be understood in the full concrete significance of the historical reality of a living man. And so, without in any way contradicting what has been said so far, it is only the concrete action and suffering of this man Jesus Christ which will make it possible to understand what love is. The name of Jesus Christ, in which God reveals Himself, gives the explanation of itself in the life and the words of Jesus Christ. For, after all, the New Testament does not consist in an endless repetition of the name of Jesus Christ, but that which this name comprises is displayed in events, concepts, and principles which are intelligible to use. And so, too, the choice of the concept of "love," is not simply arbitrary; this concept acquires an entirely new connotation in the New Testament message, yet it is not entirely without connection with what we understand by "love" in our own language. Certainly it is not true to say that the biblical concept of love is a particular form of what we have already in general understood by this word. Precisely the opposite turns out to be the case, namely, that the biblical concept of love, and it alone, is the foundation, the truth, and the reality of love, in the sense that any natural thought about love contains truth and reality only insofar as it participates in this its origin, that is to say, in the love which is God Himself in Jesus Christ.

We can now continue to follow the Bible in answering the question "What is love?" Love is the reconciliation of man with God in Jesus Christ. The disunion of men with God, with other men, with the world, and with themselves, is at an end. Man's origin is given back to him.

Love, therefore, is the name for what God does to man in overcoming the disunion in which man lives. This deed of God is Jesus Christ, is reconciliation. And so love is something which happens to man, something passive, something over which he does not himself dispose, simply because it lies beyond his existence in disunion. Love means the undergoing of the transformation of one's entire existence by God; it means being drawn into the world as it lives and must live before God and in God.

Love, therefore, is not man's choice, but it is the election of man by God.

In what sense, then, is it still possible to speak, as the New Testament does clearly enough, of love as an activity of men, of the love of men for God and for their neighbor? In view of the fact that God is love, what can now be meant by saying that man, too, can love and ought to love? "We love him, because he first loved us" (1 John 4:19). This means that our love for God rests solely upon our being loved by God, in other words, that our love can be nothing other than the willing acceptance of the love of God in Jesus Christ. "If any man love God, the same is known of him" (1 Cor. 8:3). "Known" in the language of the Bible means "elected" and "engendered." To love God means to accept willingly His election and His engendering in Christ. The relation between the divine love and human love is wrongly understood if we say that the divine love precedes the human love, but solely for the purpose of setting human love in motion as a love which, in relation to the divine love, is an independent, free, and autonomous activity of man. On the contrary, everything which is to be said of human love, too, is governed by the principle that God is love. The love with which man loves God and his neighbor is the love of God and no other; for there is no other love; there is no love which is free or independent from the love of God. In this, then, the love of men remains purely passive. Loving God is simply the other aspect of being loved by God. Being loved by God implies loving God; the two do not stand separately side by side.

In order to make this clearly intelligible a further word of explanation is necessary with regard to the use of the concept of passivity in this context. Here, as always in theology when there is reference to the passivity of men, we are not concerned with a psychological concept but with one which applies to the existence of men before God, that is to say, with a theological concept. Passivity with respect to the love of God does not mean that exclusion of all thoughts, words, and deeds which is possible when I seek repose in a love of God that can come to me only in a particular "quiet hour." The love of God is not only that haven of refuge in which I take shelter in distress. Being loved by God does not by any means deprive man of his mighty thoughts and his spirited deeds. It is as whole men, as men who think and who act, that we are loved by God and reconciled with God in Christ. And it is as whole men, who think and who act, that we love God and our brothers.

THE SUCCESSFUL MAN

Ecce homo! — Behold the man sentenced by God, the figure of grief and pain. That is how the Reconciler of the world appears. The guilt of mankind has fallen upon Him. It casts Him into shame and death before God's judgment seat. This is the great price which God pays for reconciliation with the world. Only by God's executing judgment upon Himself can there be peace between Him and the world and between man and man. But the secret of this judgment, of this passion and death, is the love of God for the world and for man. What befell Christ befalls every man in Him. It is only as one who is sentenced by God that man can live before God. Only the crucified man is at peace with God. It is in the figure of the Crucified that man recognizes and discovers himself. To be taken up by God, to be executed on the cross and reconciled, that is the reality of manhood.

In a world where success is the measure and justification of all things the figure of Him who was sentenced and crucified remains a stranger and is at best the object of pity. The world will allow itself to be subdued only by success. It is not ideas or opinions which decide, but deeds. Success alone justifies wrongs done. Success heals the wounds of guilt. There is no sense in reproaching the successful man for his unvirtuous behavior, for this would be to remain in the past while the successful man strides forward from one deed to the next, conquering the future and securing the irrevocability of what has been done. The successful man presents us with accomplished facts which can never again be reversed. What he destroys cannot be restored. What he constructs will acquire at least a prescriptive right in the next generation. No indictment can make good the guilt which the successful man has left behind him. The indictment falls silent with the passage of time, but the success remains and determines the course of history. The judges of history play a sad role in comparison with its protagonists. History rides rough-shod over their heads. With a frankness and off-handedness which no other earthly power could permit itself, history appeals in its own cause to the dictum that the end justifies the means.

So far we have been talking about facts and not about valuations. There are three possible attitudes which men and periods may adopt with regard to these facts.

When a successful figure becomes especially prominent and conspicuous, the majority give way to the idolization of success. They become blind to right and wrong, truth and untruth, fair play and foul play. They have eyes only for the deed, for the successful result. The moral and intellectual critical faculty is blunted. It is dazzled by the brilliance of the successful man and by the longing in some way to share in his success. It is not even seen that success is healing the wounds of guilt, for the guilt itself is no longer recognized. Success is simply identified with good. This attitude is genuine and pardonable only in a state of intoxication. When sobriety returns it can be achieved only at the price of a deep inner untruthfulness and conscious self-deception. This brings with it an inward rottenness from which there is scarcely a possibility of recovery.

The proposition that success is identical with good is followed by another which aims to establish the conditions for the continuance of success. This is the proposition that only good is successful. The competence of the critical faculty to judge success is reaffirmed. Now right remains right and wrong remains wrong. Now one no longer closes one's eye at the crucial moment and opens it only when the deed is done. And now there is a conscious or unconscious recognition of a law of the world, a law which makes right, truth, and order more stable in the long run than violence, falsehood, and self-will. And yet this optimistic thesis is in the end misleading. Either the historical facts have to be falsified in order to prove that evil has not been successful, which very soon brings one back to the converse proposition that success is identical with goodness, or else one's optimism breaks down in the face of the facts and one ends by finding fault with *all* historical successes.

That is why the arraigners of history never cease to complain that all success comes of wickedness. If one is engaged in fruitless and pharisaical criticism of what is past, one can never find one's way to the present, to action, and to success, and precisely in this one sees yet another proof of the wickedness of the successful man. And, if only in a negative sense, even in this one quite involuntarily makes success the measure of all things. And if success is the measure of all things, it makes no essential difference whether it is so in a positive or in a negative sense.

The figure of the Crucified invalidates all thought which takes success for its standard. Such thought is a denial of eternal justice. Neither the triumph of the successful nor the bitter hatred which the successful arouse in the hearts of the unsuccessful can ultimately overcome the world. Jesus is certainly no apologist for the successful men in history, but neither does He head the insurrection of shipwrecked existences against their successful rivals. He is not concerned with success or failure but with the willing acceptance of God's judgment. Only in this judgment is there reconciliation with God and among men. Christ confronts all thinking in terms of success and failure with the man who is under God's sentence, no matter whether he be successful or unsuccessful. It is out of pure love that God is willing to let man stand before Him, and that is why He sentences man. It is a sentence of mercy that God pronounces on mankind in Christ. In the cross of Christ God confronts the successful man with the sanctification of pain, sorrow, humility, failure, poverty, loneliness, and despair. That does not mean that all this has a value in itself, but it receives its sanctification from the love of God, the love which takes all this upon itself as its just reward. God's acceptance of the cross is His judgment upon the successful man. But the unsuccessful man must recognize that what enables him to stand before God is not his lack of success as such, not his position as a pariah, but solely the willing acceptance of the sentence passed on him by the divine love. It was precisely the cross of Christ, the failure of Christ in the world, which led to His success in history, but this is a mystery of the divine cosmic order and cannot be regarded as a general rule even though it is repeated from time to time in the sufferings of His church.

Only in the cross of Christ, that is, as those upon whom sentence has been executed, do men achieve their true form.

CONSCIENCE

It is true that it can never be advisable to act against one's own conscience. All Christian ethics is agreed in this. But what does that mean? Conscience comes from a depth which lies beyond a man's own will and his own reason and it makes itself heard as the call of human existence to unity with itself. Conscience comes as an indictment of the loss of this unity and as a warning against the loss of one's self. Primarily it is directed not toward a particular kind of doing but toward a particular mode of being. It protests against a doing which imperils the unity of this being with itself.

So long as conscience can be formally defined in these terms it is extremely inadvisable to act against its authority; disregard for the call of conscience will necessarily entail the destruction of one's own being, not even a purposeful surrender of it; it will bring about the decline and collapse of a human existence. Action against one's own conscience runs parallel with suicidal action against one's own life, and it is not by chance that the two often go together. Responsible action which did violence to conscience in this formal sense would indeed be reprehensible.

But that is not by any means the end of the question. The call of conscience arises from the imperiling of a man's unity with himself, and it is therefore now necessary to ask what constitutes this unity. The first constituent is the man's own ego in its claim to be "like God," *sicut deus,* in the knowledge of good and evil. The call of conscience in natural man is the attempt on the part of the ego to justify itself in its knowledge of good and evil before God, before men, and before itself, and to secure its own continuance in this self-justification. Finding no firm support in its own contingent individuality, the ego traces its own derivation back to the universal law of good and seeks to achieve unity with itself in conformity with this law. Thus the call of conscience has its origin and its goal in the autonomy of a man's own ego. A man's purpose in obeying this call is on each occasion anew that he should himself once more realize this autonomy which has its origin beyond his own will and knowledge "in Adam." Thus in his conscience he continues to be bound by a law of his own finding, a law which may assume different concrete forms but which he can transgress only at the price of losing his own self.

We can now understand that the great change takes place at the moment when the unity of human existence ceases to consist in its autonomy and is found, through the miracle of faith, beyond the man's own ego and its law, in Jesus Christ. The form of this change in the point of unity has an exact analogy in the secular sphere. When the national socialist says, "My conscience is Adolf Hitler," that, too, is an attempt to find a foundation for the unity of his own ego somewhere beyond himself. The consequence of this is the surrender of one's autonomy for the sake of an unconditional heteronomy, and this in turn is possible only if the other man, the man to whom I look for the unity of my life, fulfills the function of a redeemer for me. This, then, provides an extremely direct and significant parallel to the Christian truth, and at the same time an extremely direct and significant contrast with it.

When Christ, true God and true man, has become the point of unity of my existence, conscience will indeed still formally be the call of my actual being to unity with myself, but this unity cannot now be realized by means of a return to the autonomy which I derive from the law; it must be realized in fellowship with Jesus Christ. Natural conscience, no matter how strict and rigorous it may be, is now seen to be the most ungodly self-justification, and it is overcome by the conscience which is set free in Jesus Christ and which summons me to unity with myself in Jesus Christ. Jesus Christ has become my conscience. This means that I can now find unity with myself only in the surrender of my ego to God and to men. The origin and the goal of my conscience is not a law but it is the living God and the living man as he confronts me in Jesus Christ. For the sake of God and of men Jesus became a breaker of the law. He broke the law of the Sabbath in order to keep it holy in love for God and for men. He forsook His parents in order to dwell in the house of His Father and thereby to purify His obedience toward His parents. He sat at table with sinners and outcasts; and for the love of men He came to be forsaken by God in His last hour. As the one who loved without sin, He became guilty; He wished to share in the fellowship of human guilt; He rejected the devil's accusation which was intended to divert Him from this course. Thus it is Jesus Christ who sets conscience free for the service of God and of our neighbor; He sets conscience free even and especially when man enters into the fellowship of human guilt. The conscience which has been set free from the law will not be afraid to enter into the guilt of another man for the other man's sake, and indeed precisely in doing this it will show itself in its purity. The conscience which has been set free is not timid like the conscience which is bound by the law, but it stands wide open for our neighbor and for his concrete distress. And so conscience joins with the responsibility which has its foundation in Christ in bearing guilt for the sake of our neighbor. Human action is poised in a way which differs from essential original sin, yet as responsible action, in contrast to any self-righteously high-principled action, it nevertheless indirectly has a part in the action of Jesus Christ. For responsible action, therefore, there is a kind of relative freedom from sin, and this shows itself precisely in the responsible acceptance of the guilt of others.

From the principle of truthfulness Kant draws the grotesque conclusion that I must even return an honest "yes" to the enquiry of the murderer who breaks into my house and asks whether my friend whom he is pursuing has taken refuge there; in such a case self-righteousness of conscience has become outrageous presumption and blocks the path of reasonable action. Responsibility is the total and realistic response of man to the claim of God and of our neighbor; but this example shows in its true light how the response of a conscience which is bound by principles is only a partial one. If I refuse to incur guilt against the principle of truthfulness for the sake of my friend, if I refuse to tell a robust lie for the sake of my friend (for it is only the self-righteously law-abiding conscience which will pretend that, in fact, no lie is involved), if, in other words, I refuse to bear guilt for charity's sake, then my action is in contradiction to my responsibility which has its foundation in reality. Here again it is precisely in the responsible acceptance of guilt that a conscience which is bound solely to Christ will best prove its innocence....

However greatly responsibility and the conscience which is set free in Christ may desire to be united, they nevertheless continue to confront one another in a relation of irreducible tension. Conscience imposes two kinds of limit upon that bearing of guilt which from time to time becomes necessary in responsible action.

In the first place, the conscience which is set free in Christ is still essentially the summons to unity with myself. The acceptance of a responsibility must not destroy this unity. The surrender of the ego in selfless service must never be confused with the destruction and annihilation of this ego; for then indeed this ego would no longer be capable of assuming responsibility. The extent of the guilt which may be accepted in the pursuit of responsible action is on each occasion concretely limited by the requirement of the man's unity with himself, that is to say, by his carrying power. There are responsibilities which I cannot carry without breaking down under their weight; it may be a declaration of war, the violation of a political treaty, a revolution, or merely the discharge of a single employee who thereby loses the means of supporting his family; or it may be simply a piece of advice in connection with some personal decisions in life. Certainly the strength to bear responsible decisions can and should grow; certainly any failure to fulfill a responsibility is in itself a responsible decision; and yet in the concrete instance the summons of conscience to unity with oneself in Jesus Christ remains irresistible, and it is this which explains the infinite multiplicity of responsible decisions.

Secondly, even when it is set free in Jesus Christ conscience still confronts responsible action with the law, through obedience to which man is preserved in that unity with himself which has its foundation in Jesus Christ. Disregard for this law can give rise only to irresponsibility. This is the law of love for God and for our neighbor as it is explained in the decalogue, in the Sermon on the Mount, and in the apostolic parenesis. It has been correctly observed that in the contents of its law natural conscience is in strikingly close agreement with that of the conscience which has been set free in Christ. This is due to the fact that it is upon conscience that the continuance of life itself depends; conscience, therefore, contains fundamental features of the law of life, even though these features may be distorted in detail and perverted in principle. The liberated conscience is still what it was as the natural conscience, namely, the warner against transgression of the law of life. But the law is no longer the last thing; there is still Jesus Christ; for that reason, in the contest between conscience and concrete responsibility, the free decision must be given for Christ. This does not mean an everlasting conflict, but the winning of ultimate unity; for indeed the foundation, the essence, and the goal of concrete responsibility is the same Jesus Christ who is the Lord of conscience. Thus responsibility is bound by conscience, but conscience is set free by responsibility. It is now clear that it is the same thing if we say that the responsible man becomes guilty without sin or if we say that only the man with a free conscience can bear responsibility.

When a man takes guilt upon himself in responsibility, and no responsible man can avoid this, he imputes this guilt to himself and to no one else; he answers for it; he accepts responsibility for it. He does not do this in the insolent presumptuousness of his own power, but he does it in the knowledge that this liberty is forced upon him and that in this liberty he is dependent on grace. Before other men the man of free responsibility is justified by necessity; before himself he is acquitted by his conscience; but before God he hopes only for mercy.

THE CONFESSION OF GUILT

The church is precisely that community of human beings which has been led by the grace of Christ to the recognition of guilt toward Christ.... The church is that community of men which is gripped by the power of the grace of Christ so that, recognizing as guilt toward Jesus Christ both its own personal sin and the apostasy of the Western world from Jesus Christ, it confesses this guilt and accepts the burden of it. It is in her that Jesus realizes His form in the midst of the world. That is why the church alone can be the place of personal and collective rebirth and renewal....

The church confesses that she has not proclaimed often and clearly enough her message of the one God who has revealed Himself for all times in Jesus Christ and who suffers no other gods beside Himself. She confesses her timidity, her evasiveness, her dangerous concessions. She has often been untrue to her office of guardianship and to her office of comfort. And through this she has often denied to the outcast and to the despised the compassion which she owes them. She was silent when she should have cried out because the blood of the innocent was crying aloud to heaven. She has failed to speak the right word in the right way and at the right time. She has not resisted to the uttermost the apostasy of faith, and she has brought upon herself the guilt of the godlessness of the masses.

The church confesses that she has taken in vain the name of Jesus Christ, for she has been ashamed of this name before the world, and she has not striven forcefully enough against the misuse of this name for an evil purpose. She has stood by while violence and wrong were being committed under cover of this name. And indeed she has left uncontradicted, and has thereby abetted, even open mockery of the most holy name....

The church confesses that she has witnessed the lawless application of brutal force, the physical and spiritual suffering of countless innocent people, oppression, hatred, and murder, and that she has not raised her voice on behalf of the victims and has not found ways to hasten to their aid. She is guilty of the deaths of the weakest and most defenseless brothers of Jesus Christ....

The church confesses that she has witnessed in silence the spoliation and exploitation of the poor and the enrichment and corruption of the strong.

The church confesses herself guilty toward the countless victims of calumny, denunciation, and defamation. She has not convicted the slanderer of his wrongdoing, and she has thereby abandoned the slandered to his fate.

The church confesses that she has desired security, peace and quiet, possessions and honor, to which she had no right, and that in this way she has not bridled the desires of men but has stimulated them still further.

The church confesses herself guilty of breaking all ten commandments, and in this she confesses her defection from Christ. She has not borne witness to the truth of God in such a manner that all pursuit of truth, all science, can perceive that it has its origin in this truth. She has not proclaimed the justice of God in such a manner that all true justice must see in it the origin of its own essential nature. She has not succeeded in making the providence of God a matter of such certain belief that all human economy must regard it as the source from which it receives its task. By her own silence she has rendered herself guilty of the decline in responsible action, in bravery in the defense of a cause, and in willingness to suffer for what is known to be right. She bears the guilt of the defection of the governing authority from Christ.

Is this saying too much? Will some entirely blameless people stand up at this point and try to prove that it is not the church which is guilty but the others? Are there perhaps some churchmen who would reject all this as mere insulting abuse, who set themselves up to be more competent judges of the world, and who weigh up and apportion the guilt this way and that? Was not the church hindered and tied on all sides? Did not the entire secular force stand against her? Had the church the right to jeopardize her last remaining asset, her public worship and her parish life, by taking up the struggle against the anti-Christian powers? This is the voice of unbelief, which sees in the confession of guilt only a dangerous moral derogation and which fails to see that the confession of guilt is the reattainment of the form of Jesus Christ who bore the sin of the world. For indeed the free confession of guilt is not something which can be done or left undone at will. It is the emergence of the form of Jesus Christ in the church. Either the church must willingly undergo this transformation, or else she must cease to be the church of Christ. If anyone stifles or corrupts the church's confession of guilt, his guilt toward Christ is beyond hope.

By her confession of guilt the church does not exempt men from their own confession of guilt, but she calls them into the fellowship of the confession of guilt. Apostate humanity can endure before Christ only if it has fallen under the sentence of Christ. It is to this judgment that the church summons all those who hear her message.

7

After Ten Years:
A Reckoning Made
at New Year 1943

Bonhoeffer wrote these reflections for a few of his fellow con-
spirators and close family members involved in the conspiracy
against Hitler. A copy was preserved under the roof-beams
of Bonhoeffer's parents' house. It was published in his post-
humous Letters and Papers from Prison.

Ten years is a long time in anyone's life. As time is the most
valuable thing that we have, because it is the most irrevocable,
the thought of any lost time troubles us whenever we look back.
Time lost is time in which we have failed to live a full human life,
gain experience, learn, create, enjoy, and suffer; it is time that has
not been filled up, but left empty. These last years have certainly
not been like that. Our losses have been great and immeasurable,
but time has not been lost. It is true that the knowledge and
experience that were gained, and of which one did not become
conscious till later, are only abstractions of reality, of life actually lived. But just as the capacity to forget is a gift of grace, so
memory, the recalling of lessons we have learned, is also part of
responsible living....

No Ground under Our Feet

One may ask whether there have ever before in human history been people with so little ground under their feet — people to whom every available alternative seemed equally intolerable, repugnant, and futile, who looked beyond all these existing alternatives for the source of their strength so entirely in the past or in the future, and who yet, without being dreamers, were able to await the success of their cause so quietly and confidently. Or perhaps one should rather ask whether the responsible thinking people of any generation that stood at a turning point in history did not feel much as we do, simply because something new was emerging that could not be seen in the existing alternatives.

Who Stands Fast?

The great masquerade of evil has played havoc with all our ethical concepts. For evil to appear disguised as light, charity, historical necessity, or social justice is quite bewildering to anyone brought up on our traditional ethical concepts, while for the Christian who bases his life on the Bible it merely confirms the fundamental wickedness of evil.

The *"reasonable"* people's failure is obvious. With the best intentions and a naïve lack of realism, they think that with a little reason they can bend back into position the framework that has got out of joint. In their lack of vision they want to do justice to all sides, and so the conflicting forces wear them down with nothing achieved. Disappointed by the world's unreasonableness, they see themselves condemned to ineffectiveness; they step aside in resignation or collapse before the stronger party.

Still more pathetic is the total collapse of moral *fanaticism*. The fanatic thinks that his single-minded principles qualify him to do battle with the powers of evil; but like a bull he rushes at the red cloak instead of the person who is holding it; he exhausts himself and is beaten. He gets entangled in nonessentials and falls into the trap set by cleverer people.

Then there is the man with a *conscience*, who fights single-handed against heavy odds in situations that call for a decision. But the scale of the conflicts in which he has to choose — with no advice or support except from his own conscience — tears him to pieces. Evil approaches him in so many respectable and seductive disguises that his conscience becomes nervous and vacillating, till at last he contents himself with a salved instead of a clear conscience, so that he lies to his own conscience in order to avoid despair; for a man whose only support is his conscience can never realize that a bad conscience may be stronger and more wholesome than a deluded one.

From the perplexingly large number of possible decisions, the way of *duty* seems to be the sure way out. Here, what is commanded is accepted as what is most certain, and the responsibility for it rests on the commander, not on the person commanded. But no one who confines himself to the limits of duty ever goes so far as to venture, on his sole responsibility, to act in the only way that makes it possible to score a direct hit on evil and defeat it. The man of duty will in the end have to do his duty by the devil too.

As to the man who asserts his complete *freedom* to stand foursquare to the world, who values the necessary deed more highly than an unspoiled conscience or reputation, who is ready to sacrifice a barren principle for a fruitful compromise, or the barren wisdom of a middle course for a fruitful radicalism — let him beware lest his freedom should bring him down. He will assent to what is bad so as to ward off something worse, and in doing so he will no longer be able to realize that the worse, which he wants to avoid, might be the better. Here we have the raw material of tragedy.

Here and there people flee from public altercation into the sanctuary of private *virtuousness*. But anyone who does this must shut his mouth and his eyes to the injustice around him. Only at the cost of self-deception can he keep himself pure from the contamination arising from responsible action. In spite of all that he does, what he leaves undone will rob him of his peace of mind. He will either go to pieces because of this disquiet, or become the most hypocritical of Pharisees.

Who stands fast? Only the man whose final standard is not his reason, his principles, his conscience, his freedom, or his virtue, but who is ready to sacrifice all this when he is called to obedient and responsible action in faith and in exclusive allegiance to God — the responsible man, who tries to make his whole life an answer to the question and call of God. Where are these responsible people?

Of Success

Although it is certainly not true that success justifies an evil deed and shady means, it is impossible to regard success as something that is ethically quite neutral. The fact is that historical success creates a basis for the continuance of life, and it is still a moot point whether it is ethically more responsible to take the field like a Don Quixote against a new age, or to admit one's defeat, accept the new age, and agree to serve it. In the last resort success makes history; and the ruler of history repeatedly brings good out of evil over the heads of the history-makers.... To talk of going down fighting like heroes in the face of certain defeat is not really heroic at all, but merely a refusal to face the future. The ultimate question for a responsible man to ask is not how he is to extricate himself heroically from the affair, but how the coming generation is to live. It is only from this question, with its responsibility toward history, that fruitful solutions can come, even if for the time being they are very humiliating. In short, it is much easier to see a thing through from the point of view of abstract principle than from that of concrete responsibility. The rising generation will always instinctively discern which of these we make the basis of our actions, for it is their own future that is at stake....

A Few Articles of Faith on the Sovereignty of God in History

I believe that God can and will bring good out of evil, even out of the greatest evil. For that purpose he needs men who make the best use of everything. I believe that God will give us all the strength we need to help us to resist in all times of distress. But he never gives it in advance, lest we should rely on ourselves and not on him alone. A faith such as this should allay all our fears for the future. I believe that even our mistakes and shortcomings are turned to good account, and that it is no harder for God to deal with them than with our supposedly good deeds. I believe that God is no timeless fate, but that he waits for and answers sincere prayers and responsible actions.

Present and Future

We used to think that one of the inalienable rights of man was that he should be able to plan both his professional and his private life. That is a thing of the past. The force of circumstances has brought us into a situation where we have to give up being "anxious about tomorrow" (Matt. 6:34). But it makes all the difference whether we accept this willingly and in faith (as the Sermon on the Mount intends), or under continual constraint. For most people, the compulsory abandonment of planning for the future means that they are forced back into living just for the moment, irresponsibly, frivolously, or resignedly; some few dream longingly of better times to come, and try to forget the present. We find both these courses equally impossible, and there remains for us only the very narrow way, often extremely difficult to find, of living every day as if it were our last, and yet living in faith and responsibility as though there were to be a great future: "Houses and fields and vineyards shall again be bought in this land," proclaims Jeremiah (32:15), in paradoxical contrast to his prophecies of woe, just before the destruction of the holy city. It is a sign from God and a pledge of a fresh start and a great future, just when all seems black. Thinking and acting for the sake of the coming generation, but being ready to go any day without fear or anxiety — that, in practice, is the spirit in which we are forced to live. It is not easy to be brave and keep that spirit alive, but it is imperative.

Insecurity and Death

In recent years we have become increasingly familiar with the thought of death. We surprise ourselves by the calmness with which we hear of the death of one of our contemporaries. We cannot hate it as we used to, for we have discovered some good in it, and have almost come to terms with it. Fundamentally, we feel that we really belong to death already, and that every new day is a miracle. It would probably not be true to say that we welcome death (although we all know that weariness which we ought to avoid like the plague); we are too inquisitive for that — or, to put it more seriously, we should like to see something more of the meaning of our life's broken fragments. Nor do we try to romanticize death, for life is too great and too precious. Still less do we suppose that danger is the meaning of life — we are not desperate enough for that, and we know too much about the good things that life has to offer, though on the other hand we are only too familiar with life's anxieties and with all the other destructive effects of prolonged personal insecurity. We still love life, but I do not think that death can take us by surprise now. After what we have been through during the war, we hardly dare admit that we should like death to come to us, not accidentally and suddenly through some trivial cause, but in the fullness of life and with everything at stake. It is we ourselves, and not outward circumstances, who make death what it can be, a death freely and voluntarily accepted.

Are We Still of Any Use?

We have been silent witnesses of evil deeds; we have been drenched by many storms; we have learned the arts of equivocation and pretense; experience has made us suspicious of others and kept us from being truthful and open; intolerable conflicts have worn us down and even made us cynical. Are we still of any use? What we shall need is not geniuses, or cynics, or misanthropes, or clever tacticians, but plain, honest, straightforward men. Will our inward power of resistance be strong enough, and our honesty with ourselves remorseless enough, for us to find our way back to simplicity and straightforwardness?

The View from Below

There remains an experience of incomparable value. We have for once learned to see the great events of world history from below, from the perspective of the outcast, the suspects, the maltreated, the powerless, the oppressed, the reviled — in short, from the perspective of those who suffer. The important thing is that neither bitterness nor envy should have gnawed at the heart during this time, that we should have come to look with new eyes at matters great and small, sorrow and joy, strength and weakness, that our perception of generosity, humanity, justice, and mercy should have become clearer, freer, less corruptible. We have to learn that personal suffering is a more effective key, a more rewarding principle for exploring the world in thought and action than personal good fortune. This perspective from below must not become the partisan possession of those who are eternally dissatisfied; rather, we must do justice to life in all its dimensions from a higher satisfaction, whose foundation is beyond any talk of "from below" or "from above." This is the way in which we may affirm it.

8

Letters and Papers from Prison

To His Parents

[Tegel] November 27, 1943

The fact that the horrors of war are now coming home to us with such force will no doubt, if we survive, provide us with the necessary basis for making it possible to reconstruct the life of the nations, both spiritually and materially, on Christian principles. So we must try to keep these experiences in our minds, use them in our work, make them bear fruit, and not just shake them off. Never have we been so plainly conscious of the wrath of God, and that is a sign of his grace: "O that today you would hearken to his voice! Harden not your hearts." The tasks that confront us are immense, but we must prepare ourselves for them now and be ready when they come.

To Eberhard Bethge

[Tegel] December 5, 1943

My thoughts and feelings seem to be getting more and more like those of the Old Testament, and in recent months I have been reading the Old Testament much more than the New. It is only when one knows the unutterability of the name of God that one can utter the name of Jesus Christ; it is only when one loves life and the earth so much that without them everything seems to be over that one may believe in the resurrection and a new

world; it is only when one submits to God's law that one may
speak of grace; and it is only when God's wrath and vengeance
are hanging as grim realities over the heads of one's enemies that
something of what it means to love and forgive them can touch
our hearts. In my opinion it is not Christian to want to take our
thoughts and feelings too quickly and too directly from the New
Testament. We have already talked about this several times, and
every day confirms my opinion. One cannot and must not speak
the last word before the last but one. We live in the last but one
and believe the last, don't we? . . .

To His Fiancée

[Tegel] December 13, 1943

My dearest Maria,

Without abandoning all hope that things may yet take a turn
for the better just in time, I must now write you a Christmas letter. Be brave for my sake, dearest Maria, even if this letter is your
only token of my love this Christmas-tide. We shall both experience a few dark hours — why should we disguise that from each
other? We shall ponder the incomprehensibility of our lot and
be assailed by the question of why, over and above the darkness
already enshrouding humanity, we should be subjected to the bitter anguish of a separation whose purpose we fail to understand.
How hard it is inwardly to accept what defies our understanding: how great is the temptation to feel ourselves at the mercy of
blind chance; how sinister the way in which mistrust and resent-
ment steal into our hearts at such times; and how readily we fall
prey to the childish notion that the course of our lives reposes in
human hands! And then, just when everything is bearing down
on us to such an extent that we can scarcely withstand it, the
Christmas message comes to tell us that all our ideas are wrong,
and that what we take to be evil and dark is really good and light
because it comes from God. Our eyes are at fault, that is all. God
is in the manger, wealth in poverty, light in darkness, succor in
abandonment. No evil can befall us: whatever men may do to us,
they cannot but serve the God who is secretly revealed as love

and rules the world and our lives. We must learn to say: "I know how to be abased and I know how to abound; in any and all circumstances I have learned the secret of facing plenty and hunger, abundance and want. I can do all things in him who strengthens me" (Phil. 4:12 and 13) — and this Christmas, in particular, can help us to do so. What is meant here is not stoical resistance to all extraneous occurrences, but true endurance and true rejoicing in the knowledge that Christ is with us.

Dearest Maria, let us celebrate Christmas in that way. Be as happy with the others as a person can only be at Christmas time. Don't entertain any awful imaginings of me in my cell, but remember that Christ, too, frequents prisons, and that he will not pass me by. Besides, I hope to find myself a good book for Christmas and read it in peace. May you do likewise. A little oblivion is permissible in view of everything else. First one has sincerely to overcome a sorrow, then one must learn to ignore it, and finally one is entitled to forget it; but the reverse order would be mistaken and unproductive. Dearest Maria, let's not talk of what we both feel; we know it, and every word merely makes the heart heavier. Above all, let us be careful not to feel sorry for ourselves; to do so would truly be a blasphemy on God, who means us well. For all our difficulties, let us say, with Isaiah: "Do not destroy it, for there is a blessing in it" — even in this Christmas.

I've just received your letters of November 27 and December 1, also Grandmother's. When you write as cheerfully as you did, you strike a chord in me that resonates for a long time afterward. As for your marginal note — "Nonsense!" — on Grandmother's commendation of your "development," I find it very disrespectful but very nice! I'm not in favor of such statements myself, but a grandmother undoubtedly has the right to make them. Please thank her very much for her dear letter. I sometimes suspect that later — much, much later — you yourself will write similar letters, because you resemble her more than any other member of the family. Meantime, though, I'm delighted that you write as you do, because you're yourself in your letters, and I wouldn't have anything else, just you as you are. It won't be any one special thing that makes me happy; you yourself will make me so, I know. Absolve me from talking about myself; I know I can't give you anything that will lend substance to your life other than a request to abide with me, go with me, and be my beloved wife and "helpmate," just as I shall be your loving husband.

Now do me a favor and be cheerful at this time, and let me share in all your pleasures. Convey my love and profound gratitude to your mother and my fraternal greetings to your brothers and sisters. My love to your grandmother, for whom I cherish such unchanging affection, and to the Kieckowers, to whom I am linked by so many unforgettable memories, grave and gay. I often think of Konstantin [von Kleist-Retzow]. Please give my love to the Lasbeckers, too. As for you, my beloved Maria, be greeted, embraced, and kissed by

Your Dietrich

To Eberhard Bethge

[Tegel] April 11, 1944

I heard someone say yesterday that the last years had been completely wasted as far as he was concerned. I'm very glad that I have never yet had that feeling, even for a moment. Nor have I ever regretted my decision in the summer of 1939, for I'm firmly convinced — however strange it may seem — that my life has followed a straight and unbroken course, at any rate in its outward conduct. It has been an uninterrupted enrichment of experience, for which I can only be thankful. If I were to end my life here in these conditions, that would have a meaning that I think I could understand; on the other hand, everything might be a thorough preparation for a new start and a new task when peace comes.

To Eberhard Bethge

[Tegel] April 30, 1944

You would be surprised, and perhaps even worried, by my theological thoughts and the conclusion that they lead to; and this is where I miss you most of all, because I don't know anyone else with whom I could so well discuss them to have my thinking clarified. What is bothering me incessantly is the question what Christianity really is, or indeed who Christ really is, for us today. The time when people could be told everything by means of words, whether theological or pious, is over, and so is the time of inwardness and conscience — and that means the time of religion in general. We are moving toward a completely religionless time; people as they are now simply cannot be religious any more. Even those who honestly describe themselves as "religious" do not in the least act up to it, and so they presumably mean something quite different by "religious."

Our whole nineteen-hundred-year-old Christian preaching and theology rest on the "religious a priori" of mankind. "Christianity" has always been a form — perhaps the true form — of "religion." But if one day it becomes clear that this a priori does not exist at all, but was a historically conditioned and transient form of human self-expression, and if therefore man becomes radically religionless — and I think that that is already more or less the case (else how is it, for example, that this war, in contrast to all previous ones, is not calling forth any "religious" reaction?) — what does that mean for "Christianity"? It means that the foundation is taken away from the whole of what has up to now been our "Christianity," and that there remain only a few "last survivors of the age of chivalry," or a few intellectually dishonest people, on whom we can descend as "religious." Are they to be the chosen few? Is it on this dubious group of people that we are to pounce in fervor, pique, or indignation, in order to sell them our goods? Are we to fall upon a few unfortunate people in their hour of need and exercise a sort of religious compulsion on them? If we don't want to do all that, if our final judgment must be that the Western form of Christianity, too, was only a preliminary stage to a complete absence of religion, what kind of situation emerges for us, for the church? How can Christ become the Lord of the religionless as well? Are there religionless Christians? If religion is only a garment of Christianity — and even this garment has looked very different at different times — then what is a religionless Christianity?

Barth, who is the only one to have started along this line of thought, did not carry it to completion, but arrived at a positivism of revelation, which in the last analysis is essentially a restoration. For the religionless working man (or any other man) nothing decisive is gained here. The questions to be answered would surely be: What do a church, a community, a sermon, a liturgy, a Christian life mean in a religionless world? How do we speak of God — without religion, i.e., without the temporally conditioned presuppositions of metaphysics, inwardness, and so on? How do we speak (or perhaps we cannot now even "speak" as we used to) in a "secular" way about "God"? In what way are we "religionless-secular" Christians, in what way are we the ἐκ-κλησία, those who are called forth, not regarding ourselves from a religious point of view as specially favored, but rather as belonging wholly to the world? In that case Christ is no longer an object of religion, but something quite different, really the Lord of the world. But what does that mean? What is the place of worship and prayer in a religionless situation? Does the secret discipline, or alternatively the difference (which I have suggested to you before) between penultimate and ultimate, take on a new importance here? ...

The Pauline question whether [circumcision] is a condition of justification seems to me in present-day terms to be whether religion is a condition of salvation. Freedom from [circumcision] is also freedom from religion. I often ask myself why a "Christian instinct" often draws me more to the religionless people than to the religious, by which I don't in the least mean with any evangelizing intention, but, I might almost say, "in brotherhood." While I'm often reluctant to mention God by name to religious people — because that name somehow seems to me here not to ring true, and I feel myself to be slightly dishonest (it's particularly bad when others start to talk in religious jargon; I then dry up almost completely and feel awkward and uncomfortable) — to people with no religion I can on occasion mention him by name quite calmly and as a matter of course. Religious people speak of

God when human knowledge (perhaps simply because they are too lazy to think) has come to an end, or when human resources fail — in fact it is always the *deus ex machina* that they bring on to the scene, either for the apparent solution of insoluble problems, or as strength in human failure — always, that is to say, exploiting human weakness or human boundaries. Of necessity, that can go on only till people can by their own strength push these boundaries somewhat further out, so that God becomes superfluous as a *deus ex machina*. I've come to be doubtful of talking about any human boundaries (is even death, which people now hardly fear, and is sin, which they now hardly understand, still a genuine boundary today?). It always seems to me that we are trying anxiously in this way to reserve some space for God; I should like to speak of God not on the boundaries but at the center, not in weaknesses but in strength; and therefore not in death and guilt but in man's life and goodness. As to the boundaries it seems to me better to be silent and leave the insoluble, unsolved. Belief in the resurrection is *not* the "solution" of the problem of death. God's "beyond" is not the beyond of our cognitive faculties. The transcendence of epistemological theory has nothing to do with the transcendence of God. God is beyond in the midst of our life. The church stands, not at the boundaries where human powers give out, but in the middle of the village. That is how it is in the Old Testament, and in this sense we still read the New Testament far too little in the light of the Old. How this religionless Christianity looks, what form it takes, is something that I'm thinking about a great deal, and I shall be writing to you again about it soon. It may be that on us in particular, midway between East and West, there will fall a heavy responsibility.

Who Am I?

Who am I? They often tell me
I would step from my cell's confinement
calmly, cheerfully, firmly,
like a squire from his country-house.

Who am I? They often tell me
I would talk to my warders
freely and friendly and clearly,
as though it were mine to command.

Who am I? They also tell me
I would bear the days of misfortune
equably, smilingly, proudly,
like one accustomed to win.

Am I then really all that which other men tell of?
Or am I only what I know of myself,
restless and longing and sick, like a bird in a cage,
struggling for breath, as though hands were compressing my
     throat,
yearning for colors, for flowers, for the voices of birds,
thirsting for words of kindness, for neighborliness,
trembling with anger at despotisms and petty humiliation,
tossing in expectation of great events,
powerlessly trembling for friends at an infinite distance,
weary and empty at praying, at thinking, at making,
faint, and ready to say farewell to it all?

Who am I? This or the other?
Am I one person today, and tomorrow another?
Am I both at once? A hypocrite before others,
and before myself a contemptibly woebegone weakling?
Or is something within me still like a beaten army,
fleeing in disorder from victory already achieved?

Who am I? They mock me, these lonely questions of mine.
Whoever I am, thou knowest, O God, I am thine.

To Eberhard Bethge

                                                   July 18, 1944

I wonder whether any letters have been lost in the raids on Munich. Did you get the one with the two poems? It was just sent

off that evening, and it also contained a few introductory remarks on our theological theme. The poem about Christians and pagans contains an idea that you will recognize: "Christians stand by God in his hour of grieving"; that is what distinguishes Christians from pagans. Jesus asked in Gethsemane, "Could you not watch with me one hour?" That is a reversal of what the religious man expects from God. Man is summoned to share in God's sufferings at the hands of a godless world.

He must therefore really live in the godless world, without attempting to gloss over or explain its ungodliness in some religious way or other. He must live "secular" life, and thereby share in God's sufferings. He *may* live a "secular" life (as one who has been freed from false religious obligations and inhibitions). To be a Christian does not mean to be religious in a particular way, to make something of oneself (a sinner, a penitent, or a saint) on the basis of some method or other, but to be a man — not a type of man, but the man that Christ creates in us. It is not the religious act that makes the Christian, but participation in the sufferings of God in the secular life.

To Eberhard Bethge

[Tegel] July 21 [1944]

During the last year or so I've come to know and understand more and more the profound this-worldliness of Christianity. The Christian is not a *homo religiosus,* but simply a man, as Jesus was a man — in contrast, shall we say, to John the Baptist. I don't mean the shallow and banal this-worldliness of the enlightened, the busy, the comfortable, or the lascivious, but the profound this-worldliness, characterized by discipline and the constant knowledge of death and resurrection. I think Luther lived a this-worldly life in this sense.

I remember a conversation that I had in America thirteen years ago with a young French pastor. We were asking ourselves quite simply what we wanted to do with our lives. He said he would like to become a saint (and I think it's quite likely that he did become one). At the time I was very impressed, but I disagreed with him, and said, in effect, that I should like to learn to have faith. For a long time I didn't realize the depth of the contrast. I thought I could acquire faith by trying to live a holy life, or something like it. I suppose I wrote *The Cost of Discipleship* as the end of that path. Today I can see the dangers of that book, though I still stand by what I wrote.

I discovered later, and I'm still discovering right up to this moment, that it is only by living completely in this world that one learns to have faith. One must completely abandon any attempt to make something of oneself, whether it be a saint, or a converted sinner, or a churchman (a so-called priestly type!), a righteous man or an unrighteous once; a sick man or a healthy one. By this-worldliness I mean living unreservedly in life's duties, problems, successes and failures, experiences and perplexities. In so doing we throw ourselves completely into the arms of God, taking seriously, not our own sufferings, but those of God in the world — watching with Christ in Gethsemane. That, I think, is faith; that is *metanoia;* and that is how one becomes a man and a Christian (cf. Jer. 45!). How can success make us arrogant, or failure lead us astray, when we share in God's sufferings through a life of this kind?

Stations on the Road to Freedom

DISCIPLINE

If you set out to seek freedom, then learn above all things
to govern your soul and your senses, for fear that your passions
and longing may lead you away from the path you should follow.
Chaste be your mind and your body, and both in subjection,
obediently, steadfastly seeking the aim set before them;
only through discipline may a man learn to be free.

ACTION

Daring to do what is right, not what fancy may tell you,
valiantly grasping occasions, nor cravenly doubting —

freedom comes only through deeds, not through thoughts taking
  wing.
Faint not nor fear, but go out to the storm and the action,
trusting in God whose commandment you faithfully follow;
freedom, exultant, will welcome your spirit with joy.

SUFFERING

A change has come indeed. Your hands, so strong and active,
are bound; in helplessness now you see your action
is ended; you sigh in relief, your cause committing
to stronger hands; so now you may rest contented.
Only for one blissful moment could you draw near to touch
  freedom;
then, that it might be perfected in glory, you gave it to God.

DEATH

Come now, thou greatest of feasts on the journey to freedom
  eternal;
death, cast aside all the burdensome chains, and demolish
the walls of our temporal body, the walls of our souls that are
  blinded,
so that at last we may see that which here remains hidden.
Freedom, how long we have sought thee in discipline, action,
  and suffering;
dying, we now may behold thee revealed in the Lord.

To Eberhard Bethge

[Tegel] August 21, 1944

In these turbulent times we repeatedly lose sight of what really
makes life worth living. We think that, because this or that person
is living, it makes sense for us to live too. But the truth is that if
this earth was good enough for the man Jesus Christ, if such a
man as Jesus lived, then, and only then, has life a meaning for
us. If Jesus had not lived, then our life would be meaningless, in
spite of all the other people whom we know and honor and love.

Perhaps we now sometimes forget the meaning and purpose of our profession. But isn't this the simplest way of putting it? The unbiblical idea of "meaning" is indeed only a translation of what the Bible calls "promise."

To Eberhard Bethge

[Tegel] 23 [August 1944]

Please don't ever get anxious or worried about me, but don't forget to pray for me — I'm sure you don't! I am so sure of God's guiding hand that I hope I shall always be kept in that certainty. You must never doubt that I'm traveling with gratitude and cheerfulness along the road where I'm being led. My past life is brimful of God's goodness, and my sins are covered by the forgiving love of Christ crucified. I'm most thankful for the people I have met, and I only hope that they never have to grieve about me, but that they, too, will always be certain of, and thankful for, God's mercy and forgiveness. Forgive my writing this. Don't let it grieve or upset you for a moment, but let it make you happy. But I did want to say it for once, and I couldn't think of anyone else who I could be sure would take it aright.

To His Mother

[Prinz-Albrecht-Strasse] December 28, 1944

Dear Mother,

I'm so glad to have just got permission to write you a birthday letter. I have to write in some haste, as the post is just going. All I really want to do is to help to cheer you a little in these days that you must be finding so bleak. Dear Mother, I want you to know that I am constantly thinking of you and Father every day, and that I thank God for all that you are to me and the whole family. I know you've always lived for us and haven't lived a life of your own. That is why you're the only one with whom I can share all that I'm going through. It's a very great comfort to me that Maria is with you. Thank you for all the love that has come to

THE SPIRITUAL MASTERS SERIES

These volumes are now available through your bookseller or direct from Orbis Books.

Henri Nouwen
edited with an Introduction by Robert A. Jonas
ISBN: 1-57075-197-8 $14.00

Simone Weil
edited with an Introduction by Eric O. Springsted
ISBN: 1-57075-204-4 $13.00

To order direct with a Mastercard or VISA, call toll-free 1-800-258-5838, Monday-Friday 8:30-3:30 Eastern Time, or e-mail via our Web page http://www.maryknoll.org/orbis/mklorbhp.html, or copy this page and mail

ORBIS BOOKS
Walsh Building
P.O. Box 308
Maryknoll, N.Y. 10545-0308.

Titles subject to availability. Prices subject to change.

me in my cell from you during the past year, and has made every day easier for me. I think these hard years have brought us closer together than we ever were before. My wish for you and Father and Maria and for us all is that the New Year may bring us at least an occasional glimmer of light, and that we may once more have the joy of being together. May God keep you both well.

With most loving wishes, dear, dear Mother, for a happy birthday.

Your grateful Dietrich